CAROLYN WARRENDER'S
BOOK OF
Colour
SCHEMING

CAROLYN WARRENDER'S BOOK OF
Colour
SCHEMING

HarperCollins*Publishers*

Published for
The Regent Academy of Fine Arts
London

by
HarperCollins*Publishers*
Published 1998

Special photography by Shona Wood
Colour wheel illustrations by Cherrill Parris
Practical illustrations by John Hutchinson
Picture research by Julia Pashley

A catalogue record for this book is available from the British Library

ISBN 0261 670441

Colour reproduction in Singapore by Colourscan
Printed and bound in Scotland

CONTENTS

INTRODUCTION

Imagine that you are returning home after a long summer holiday. What happens when you turn the key in the lock and walk around the house or apartment, making sure that everything is in place? Do you feel a sense of satisfaction and well-being as you move from room to room, or does a checklist start to form in your mind – I need to replace that carpet; I must do something about the lighting in the living room; how can I make the kitchen more cheerful? As likely as not, you will experience a mixture of positive and negative emotions as you make your tour. Most of us decorate our homes over a period of several years and, during that time, new styles and fashions influence us. We also make fresh discoveries about ourselves. Even the most seasoned interior designer will look for ways to alter and improve her home as she moves around it.

Home decoration is an ongoing process. In this book, I hope to share with you the ways in which I have made that process one that is rich in adventure, enjoyment and discovery. My starting point, and the point to which I return again and again, is colour. How can the homemaker of today make the most of colour? There is certainly no shortage of material with which to experiment – if anything, there is too much. Decorating shops offer the consumer a dazzling range of paints, wallpapers, soft furnishing fabrics, stencil patterns, carpets, rugs and storage systems. What's more, there is a huge range of international styles on the market. Today's buyer can select tables from Singapore, beds and wardrobes from Scandinavia, Shaker-style kitchens, Mediterranean-style bathrooms. With such a vast array of colours and traditions to choose from, it can be extremely hard to establish your own personal style. How can you experiment with the materials that are on the market without making costly mistakes and ending up with a jumble of styles? And how can you acquire the skills that will give you the confidence to create a house which reflects your particular personality and taste?

I believe that you, and anyone else, can acquire these skills by learning, first, what colours will work best for you and secondly, how to combine these colours so that they bring out the best features in your home. Just as you are likely to feel more cheerful and confident in clothes whose colour and style flatter you, so you are likely to feel more at ease in surroundings that enhance you.

The first step is to establish your colour palette. When I use colour in interior design, I take my inspiration from the natural world. The elements of nature seem to provide everything you need to create colour schemes that are harmonious, versatile and enjoyable to live with. So the seven palettes I use are all based on the elements. They are:

The Natural Palette, The Air Palette, The Wind Palette, The Water Palette, The Fire Palette, The Earth Palette and The Mineral Palette.

Within each of these palettes, the colours are subdivided into warm-based and cool-based. Warm-based colours have a yellow base, while cool-based colours have a blue base. And by studying the first chapter of this book and then completing the questionnaire on pages 124-5, you will be able to ascertain which colour palette is the best for you. With this as your foundation, you will know how to make the most of the information in Living with Colour, the central section of the book (see page 62). Here, you will learn about the way in which colour, light and texture interact with each other; and you will be shown how to experiment with different colours and textures by making your own sample boards. You will also learn how to view your house as a whole, and so create a colour scheme which is coordinated in an overall sense. Then, a room-by-room analysis will show you how the different components of a room can be combined in colourways that work alongside each other so as to achieve a particular atmosphere. For each room in the house, a step-by-step project will enable you to create some of these effects for yourself, without needing to employ an interior designer.

If you would like to learn more about the uses of colour in a workshop situation, please contact me at the address given on page 128. In the meantime, I hope that this book will give you the skills you need to use colour with confidence, flair and pleasure and that it will be both a source of inspiration and a practical reference work for many years to come.

Carolyn Warrender

Understanding Colour

Colour has a language which is not difficult to master. You can quickly learn the principles that have been discovered by major artists and colour theorists in previous eras and apply them to interior design. Whatever your budget, you can use colour to transform the dreariest of rooms into a place fit for a queen. Today more than ever before, you have the advantage of a wonderful range of fabrics, paints, wallpapers and accessories. Once you have learnt the basic rules of colour and identified your own palette, you will be able to use this rich array of materials with flair, confidence and natural good taste.

UNDERSTANDING COLOUR

When we perceive different colours, what we are really seeing is light reflected back to our eyes in different wavelengths from the variety of surfaces around us.

THE COLOUR SPECTRUM

These wavelengths together make up the colours of the rainbow – red, orange, yellow, green, indigo and violet – traditionally regarded as comprising the colour spectrum. Red has the longest wavelength and violet the shortest, with the wavelengths of the colours in between steadily decreasing.

At either end of the spectrum are white and black. White reflects and contains all the other colours within it, as Sir Isaac Newton discovered in 1666. He used a triangular prism to catch a shaft of sunlight and found that he created a second shaft that showed each colour of the rainbow contained within the white sunlight. In contrast to white, black absorbs light. The three pigments used by printers – cyan (blue), yellow and magenta (red) – combine to create black as a fourth colour in the printing process.

PRIMARY, SECONDARY AND TERTIARY COLOURS

Just over a hundred years after Newton's discovery, the scientist and naturalist Moses Harris created in 1770 the first colour wheel to classify red, blue and yellow as the three primary colours. By the mid-nineteenth century this classification was widely accepted by artists. Then, in the early twentieth century, the German painter, teacher and art theoretician Johannes Itten extended the classification to include secondary and tertiary colours. Itten was an important personality during the early years of the German Bauhaus movement in the 1920s. The Bauhaus movement had as its aim the incorporation of art into everyday life, including industrial life. Itten played a key role in pioneering a new approach to colour. During the 1920s, he developed a colour star which included twelve colours – three primary, three secondary and six tertiary. The primary colours are so called because they cannot be created by mixing any other colours together. Then the

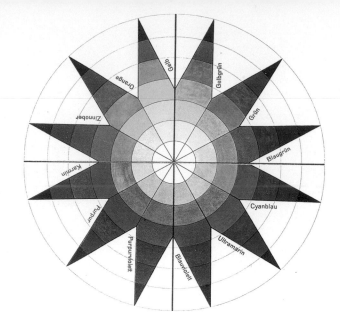

ABOVE Johannes Itten's colour star defines the twelve colours (hues) by tone (light or dark) and saturation (depth of colour).

secondary colours are made by mixing two of the primary colours together – red and yellow make orange; yellow and blue make green; and red and blue mixed together make purple. The six tertiary colours are created when two secondary colours are mixed together.

TINTS AND SHADES

Any colour can be lightened by the addition of white, when it is known as a 'tint'. The same colour can also be darkened by the addition of black, known as 'shading'. Red, when tinted with white, becomes a feminine pink; when shaded with black it turns to a more masculine burgundy. The addition of white and black to different colours is said to change that colour's tone.

COMPLEMENTARY AND HARMONIOUS COLOURS

Complementary colours have a strong visual resonance when they are placed alongside each other. Red and green, blue and yellow, orange and purple are complementaries. When you use complementary colours in interior design, you should include both colours in equal measure and of an equal intensity to achieve a balanced result. Harmonious colours rest alongside each other in the colour spectrum. Yellow and orange harmonize with each other, as do blue and purple. Experimenting with crayons is an easy way of exploring the relationship of different colours to each other and discovering which combinations you like.

LEFT This stone-flagged hallway shows four harmonious colours resting comfortably alongside each other. The wood of the staircase is close in the colour spectrum to that of the flagstones, while the pink of the wall contains sufficient beige to link the two. The white painted skirting board extends the floor area, adding light and space.

THE COLOUR PALETTES

Johannes Itten also pioneered the notion of warm and cool colours. According to Itten, any shade of colour can have either a warm base or a cool base, an insight which has considerable implications for interior designers. If you know whether you prefer a cool yellow or a warm yellow as the background colour for your room, and if you know how to extend that colour scheme according to Johannes Itten's classification, you are well on the way to creating the kind of room you want. Itten divided the colour spectrum into two complementary halves, one half comprising warm shades and the other comprising cool shades. The colour wheel shown opposite divides the shades into warm and cool colours. At the same time, it shows each of the colours at varying degrees of intensity and depth. The warm and cool halves of the wheel are subdivided into seven distinct palettes. Because much of my inspiration comes from the natural world, I call these palettes Natural, Air, Wind, Water, Fire, Earth and Mineral. Thus, within the divisions of warm and cool are:

THE NATURAL PALETTE
THE AIR PALETTE
THE WIND PALETTE
THE WATER PALETTE
THE FIRE PALETTE
THE EARTH PALETTE
THE MINERAL PALETTE

These seven colour palettes will give you the tools you need to extend your colour scheme in a way that is visually harmonious. Later in this chapter, each of the colour palettes is discussed in more detail. In the following chapter of the book, you will see many examples of colour palettes being combined in specific ways to create a wide range of effects and styles in all rooms of the home. Answering the questionnaire in the final chapter of the book will help you to find which colour palette will work best for you. For example, if the Wind Palette is most appropriate for you, it is a good idea to combine your decorating colours from the shades that are specific to that palette. In this way, you will be able to design and to

ABOVE Cool colours, based on blue undertones

decorate your home to suit your personal taste. In particular, you will be able confidently to combine a variety of colours in such a way that each room in your home is well-balanced, harmonious and a pleasure to live in. As you gain more confidence, you will find that you can combine warm and cool colours from the same palettes as well as working exclusively within one half of the spectrum. For example, you can use warm accents as highlights in a primarily cool colour scheme. Remember too that the natural palette can be combined with any of the other six.

ABOVE Warm colours, based on yellow undertones

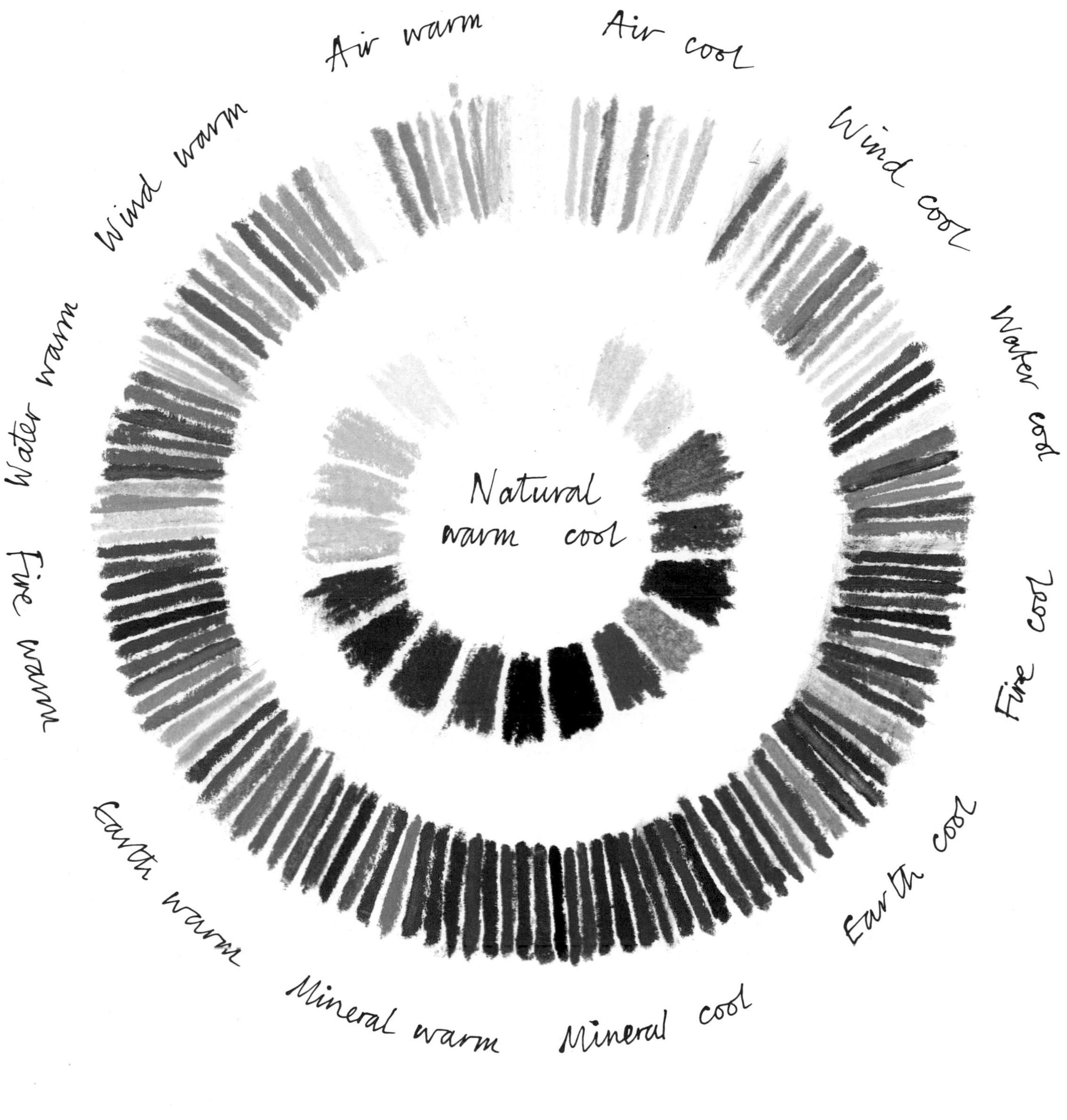

Air warm

Air cool

Wind warm

Wind cool

Water warm

Water cool

Fire warm

Fire cool

Natural
warm   cool

Earth warm

Earth cool

Mineral warm

Mineral cool

THE PROPERTIES OF COLOUR

Red

Red is a colour that advances, stimulating a response and creating an atmosphere of assertion and strength. It is associated with excitement, vitality and physical power. Because it is a colour that flatters the skin, it can make an excellent background in rooms that are used for social functions. Pale pinks are warm and peaceful and combine successfully with greens. The deeper reds can create an atmosphere of restrained opulence and power.

Orange

Midway between red and yellow, orange is essentially a cheerful colour, with a glow that can be used to good effect in north- and east-facing rooms. Since it is also an assertive and dynamic colour, it can be overpowering when used on large surfaces in interior design, though used with discretion it can create an atmosphere of vivacious spontaneity and liveliness.

Yellow

Because we tend to associate it with sunshine, yellow can appear as a light source in its own right. This makes it an effective colour for bringing a sense of natural light into urban settings; even dark yellow rooms can have an airy, radiant atmosphere. The use of yellow in any living space can create a feeling of hope and inspiration, and an optimistic sense that all is well with the world.

Green

A discreet colour, green suggests security, protection and harmony. Green also has a calming effect, making it a popular choice for bedrooms, while dark greens make excellent colours for studies and home offices. The 'green' rooms of theatres are so called because their green walls are intended to steady the nerves of actors and actresses as they prepare to go on stage and perform. Pale greens are particularly restful colours, though they can be severe on the skin; a reliable way to counteract this is by introducing rich blues and turquoises somewhere in the room as colour accents.

many shades and textures of brown that combine in the bark of a tree or the shell of a nut are infinitely rich and subtle and extraordinarily restful to look upon. Some of these qualities are captured in well-made furniture, turning the best wooden pieces into collectors' items. One characteristic of brown is that it creates a feeling of coolness and warmth at the same time. As a furnishing fabric, it combines well with rich colours such as purple and gold, a popular combination in the Victorian era.

WHITE

White promotes an air of cleanliness, simplicity and hygiene. In buildings with strong architectural features, such as exposed beams, white can be used to give these features additional emphasis. However, it is often seen as a 'safe' fallback where a stronger colour would be more effective. If you are decorating a room with a white background, you run the risk of creating a clinical atmosphere, so consider choosing an off-white such as gardenia, ivory or dove grey to create a softer and more finished look.

BLACK

Because it absorbs light, black is an exacting colour to work with in interior design. Its association with bereavement and death also makes it a morbid colour for the home. However, black accents can transform an otherwise bland interior – black picture frames and curtain rails, burgundy-black laquer and black lampshades will introduce a note of drama and sophistication into otherwise plain surroundings. Black will also punctuate colour schemes which rely on strong, contrasting colours.

BLUE

The colour of the sea and sky, blue has a quality of cool expansiveness and openness. Used in interior design, it has a relaxing and sedative effect. Blue is associated with a sense of formality, though the mid-blues also have a playful quality about them. Because of its association with water, blue is a popular colour for kitchens and bathrooms; it can also create an atmosphere of spaciousness and tranquility in reception rooms and a fresh look, combined with white, in bedrooms.

VIOLET

A combination of blue and red, violet is a regal and dignified colour that needs to be used with discretion. Pale shades of violet are restful and serene, but the darker shades can make it difficult to focus and, if used over large expanses, are tiring on the eyes. At the same time, this quality can make purple an excellent foil for works of art.

BROWN

The colour of living wood, brown is essentially an earth colour. In nature, the

A COLOUR BY ANY OTHER NAME

The human eye can recognize thousands of shades in the colours we term generically as red, yellow, blue and so on. Remember, though, that wallpaper, paint and textile manufacturers may well give products containing similar shades quite different names. When you are trying to find a colour that you like, it can be confusing to find what seems to be the same shade classified by one manufacturer as forest green, by another as jungle green, and by a third as oak green. It can also be dangerous to assume that a paint called pale apricot will complement a fabric of the same name. The best way to negotiate the maze of colour names on the market is to collect samples and make your own assessment of what colours work well with each other. The names I have chosen for the palettes described here are all inspired by the colours of nature.

LEFT Yellow is famous for its uplifting properties and is most effective in spaces that enjoy plenty of natural light. On this stairwell its effectiveness is enhanced by the yellow panes in the stained glass window.

RIGHT Red is a warm and inviting colour. It is softened by being combined with cream and given definition by being combined with black. In this sitting room, both of these combinations have been employed, with an attractive mixture of patterns adding to the overall effect.

HOW COLOUR AFFECTS US

Using colour is a two-way process. We use it to express our personalities, to make statements about how we see ourselves, and to reveal our preferences and tastes. At the same time, the colours we live with directly influence the way we feel, the efficiency with which we work and the extent to which we are able to relax. Colour can play a major part in our overall state of wellbeing. So whether you want to create a dramatic living room or a subdued bedroom, knowing how to combine different shades of colour within a colour spectrum that is almost infinitely expandable will enable you to create genuinely personal colour schemes with confidence, individuality and flair. The qualities associated with different colours are discussed on pages 14–15, but remember that the many tones of any given colour can achieve quite varied effects. For each colour, there are thousands of varieties on the market in the form of paint, wallpaper and soft furnishing fabrics. In order to achieve the look you want, you need to pay close attention to the shades of colour you select.

COLOUR AND SPACE

Colour can significantly alter the sense of space in a room. Dark shades will make a large room seem smaller, while light and neutral colours will increase the sense of space in a small room. So by choosing to decorate a room with a dark or light colour tone, you will immediately create a particular effect. Before making your choice, consider the purpose of the room you are decorating. Is this a space where you wish to create a quiet, introspective atmosphere or one that is more stimulating and lively, appropriate for entertaining? In contemporary homes, many rooms are used for more than one purpose. If you are decorating a bedroom, for example, is the room also going to function as a play area for a child, or a study area for a teenager?

COLOUR AND LIGHT

Because colour *is* light, changes in light bring about immediate changes in the colour of any object or surface. Conversely, the atmosphere of a room can be altered dramatically by the introduction of a new colour because that colour will alter the quality of light in the room. In creating a successful scheme in any room, it is essential to bear the intimate relationship between colour and light in mind. Which way does the room face? How much sunlight does it receive, and at what time of day? When is the

ABOVE In this sitting room the discipline of white and lavender dominates the colour scheme. But the use of several textures – on the rug, the chairs, the blinds, curtains and paintwork – enhances the interplay of colour and light.

room most likely to be used? To what extent does the quality of natural light in the room change from season to season? When illuminated by artificial light, how does the interplay between light and colour alter? And how do you, as the architect of the room, wish it to alter?

ABOVE The almost exclusive use of natural colours, with two glazed Japanese pots as accents, creates an atmosphere of simple elegance in this music room.

Light alone can transform a room without any other changes being necessary. It can make spaces seem larger or smaller, more functional or more intimate. By making the most of natural light, and by using artificial light not only for illumination but also for a particular effect, you can

make the same living space extraordinarily versatile. If you use your kitchen as a dining room, for example, you will need to consider how you can explore the many different ways of using light to change the mood of the room at different times of day.

COLOUR AND CONTRAST
Because of the interplay of colour and light, contrasting textures can create many pleasingly subtle effects when you are working either with the same colour or with different ones. Contrasts such as rough-smooth, pointed-blunt, light-dark, hard-soft, heavy-light can all enrich the colour treatment of an interior space.

NATURAL COLOURS
'Natural' is the term used to describe any colour in which white has been used as a tint to dilute the impact of that colour. The natural colours most often used in interior design are grey-based or brown-based. The notion of a natural red or a natural blue sounds contradictory, but if these or any other colours are predominantly white, then they can be regarded as natural too.

THE FUNCTION OF NATURALS
In many ways, naturals are the designer's best friend. Used exclusively, they create a restful, calm and undemanding ambience. As a base colour on floors, walls and ceilings, they provide a foil for the impact of more dramatic soft furnishing fabrics. Naturals can also be combined with stronger colours such as reds and oranges in patterned rugs and carpets, to bridge the contrast between a solid foreground colour, such as a red sofa, and a neutral base colour, such as dove-grey walls.

Natural colours lend a sense of space to small rooms. They can be dreary in basements or north-facing rooms, but wherever there is plenty of natural light, the dominance of white in naturals will enhance that light. Naturals will also be a good choice in any well-lit room where you want an atmosphere of spaciousness, simplicity and calm. They are excellent colours for hallways and corridors, as they will both link and punctuate the overall colour scheme in a home.

THE
NATURAL
PALETTE

Natural describes any colour in which black, brown or white is the main ingredient. The natural colours that are most often used in home furnishings are grey-based or brown-based. The natural palette is like your kitchen store cupboard. There you find the basics you need for all cooking. Look upon natural colours in the same way when planning your colour schemes. Among naturals you will find the shades that act as a foil for more intense colours. Think about how natural colours are used on a beach, with sand and pebbles acting as a base for the deep sea and rock colours. All naturals have a pleasing simplicity about them, which is perhaps the reason why they find favour in so many people's homes. If you are cautious about how to experiment with colour, the natural palette can be a good place to start. Used exclusively, these colours create a restful, calm and undemanding ambience. As a base colour on floors, walls, and ceilings, they provide a foil for the impact of more dramatic furnishings. Think too of using naturals as accents for scatter cushions, trimmings and rugs in more colourful rooms. The joy of natural colours is that they can be used with any colour you want. They lend a sense of space to small and dark rooms. Where there is plenty of natural light, they will enhance that light. Naturals will also serve you well in any well-lit room where you want an atmosphere of spaciousness, simplicity and calm. They are excellent colours for hallways and corridors, as they will both link and punctuate the overall scheme in a home.

LEFT Cool whites used across the floor, walls and ceilings dissolves angles and borders. In this room, their use also accentuates the importance of the exposed beams. The striped cushion covers add a touch of definition, but the theme here is definitely one of 'less is more'.

RIGHT Large urns with bold displays of twigs stand in this room like two silent guests. These warm natural colours and the contrasting textures of the coir matting, woodwork, sofa, stoneware and cushions give this room a marked tactile quality.

THE
AIR
PALETTE

THE AIR PALETTE

The air palette divides into warm and cool base colours.
Once you have completed the questionnaire on pages 124-5,
and have discovered if you are essentially warm- or cool-
based, use the appropriate wheel to select your colours.
These can then be used in decorating or furnishing your
room, either on their own or in combination with colours
from the warm or cool side of the other palettes.

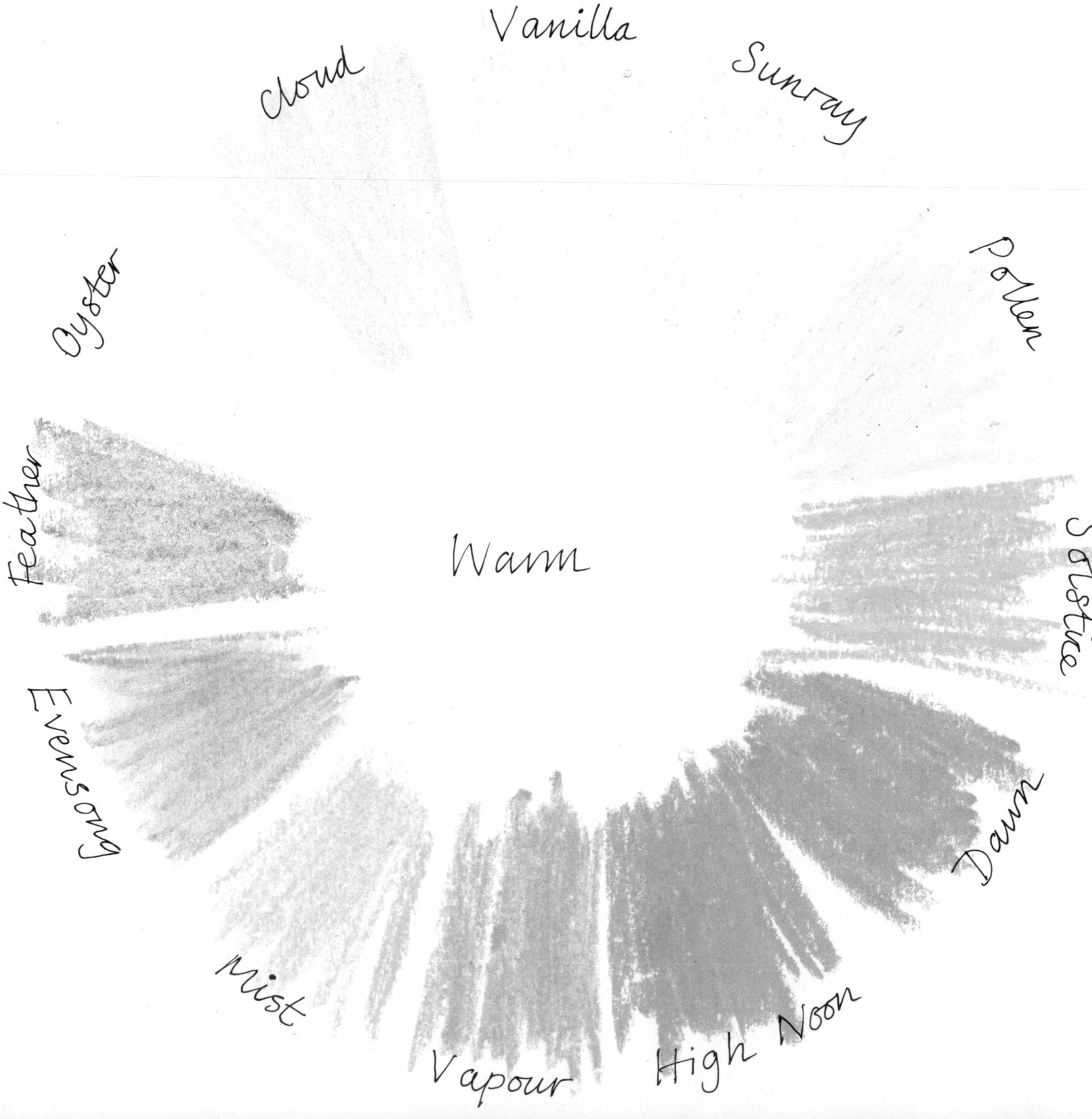

Vanilla

Cloud

Sunray

Oyster

Pollen

Feather

Solstice

Warm

Evensong

Dawn

Mist

Vapour

High Noon

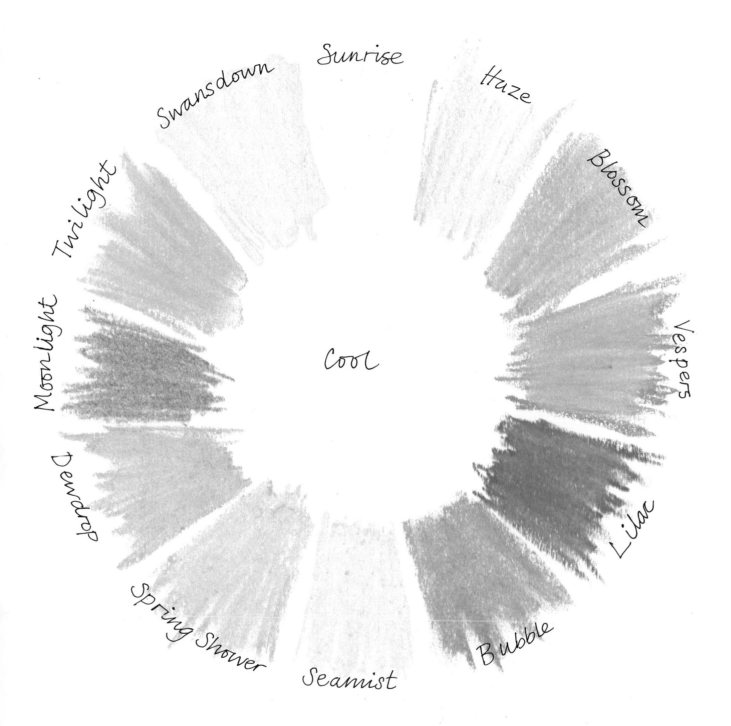

Sunrise

Swansdown

Haze

Twilight

Blossom

Moonlight

Vespers

Cool

Dewdrop

Lilac

Spring Shower

Bubble

Seamist

Air is around us all the time. We say the sky is blue, but what colour is the air itself? Like the element from which it takes its name, the air colour palette is subtle and elusive. More than any other palette, these colours are suffused with light, giving them an attractive outdoor allure with very feminine, calm and summery tones.

Among the warm air colours are Sunray, Pollen, Mist and Cloud. Among the cool air colours are Haze, Bubble, Dewdrop and Swansdown. There is a romantic association to these colours that makes them ideal for bedrooms, guest rooms and bathrooms. At the same time, the outdoor quality of the palette is suitable for garden rooms where plants can play a major role in the colour scheme. The air colours also make good companions for patterned fabrics, especially where the patterns are understated.

The delicacy of the air palette can easily be overpowered by dark colours and by heavy pieces of furniture. With these colours, consider using painted and stencilled furniture, perhaps coordinating a motif from a floral curtain or bedspread as part of your scheme. Pale woods such as ash, bamboo and pine rest well alongside the warm air colours, while limed oak complements the cool air colours on the other side of the palette. Choose lightweight curtain fabrics such as muslins, soft cottons, delicate silks and chintz to make the best of air colours.

The air palette belongs, above all, in rooms that receive plenty of natural light. If you are converting an attic space into a young girl's den, or creating a light-filled bedroom in a country cottage, this palette will help you to achieve an atmosphere that gives a sense of airy, sunny spaciousness.

RIGHT Warm yellows act as the foreground colours in this wood-panelled sitting room. The discipline of yellow and white is lightly accented by blue and green, creating the spirit of a sunny garden.

RIGHT Cool air colours create a distinctive, feminine atmosphere in this bedroom. The choice of a finely detailed pattern on the quilt and the abundance of lace pillowcases add to this effect.

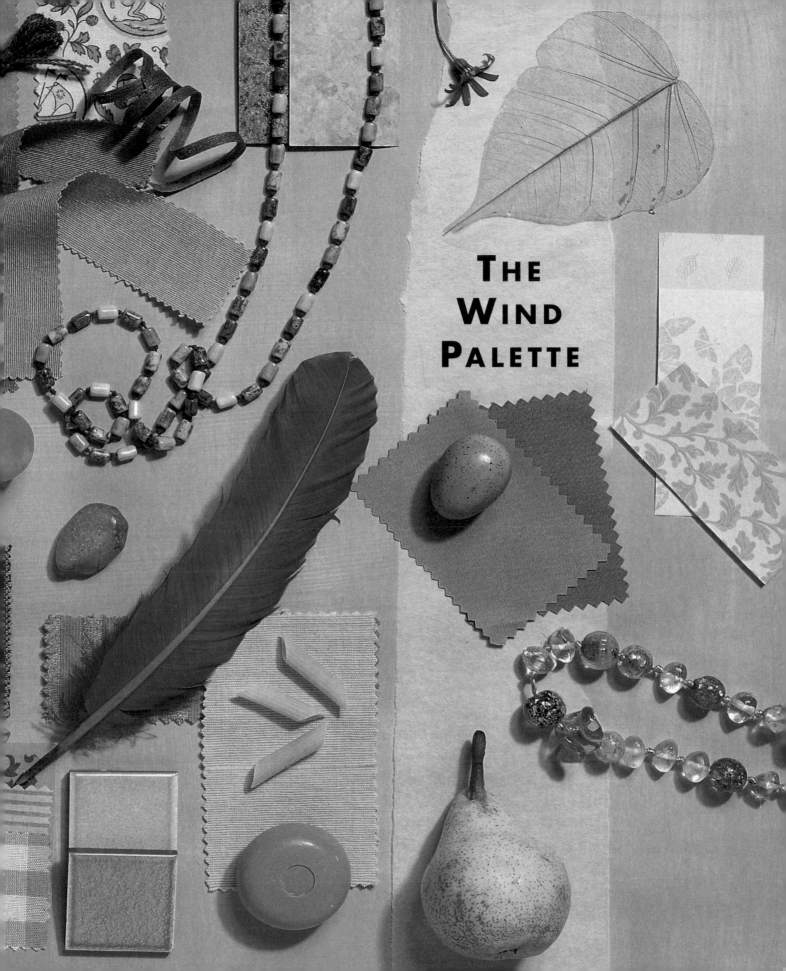

THE
WIND
PALETTE

THE WIND PALETTE

The wind palette divides into warm and cool base colours.
Once you have completed the questionnaire on pages 124-5,
and have discovered if you are essentially warm- or cool-
based, use the appropriate wheel to select your colours.
These can then be used in decorating or furnishing your
room, either on their own or in combination with colours
from the warm or cool side of the other palettes.

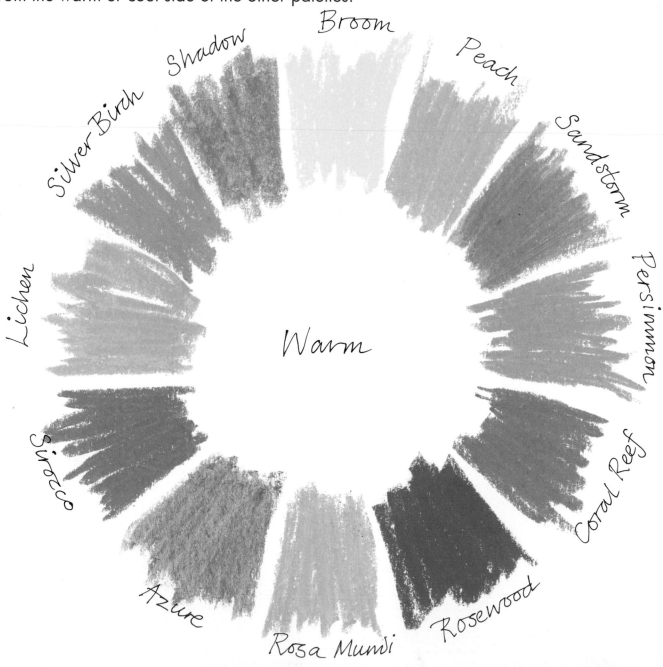

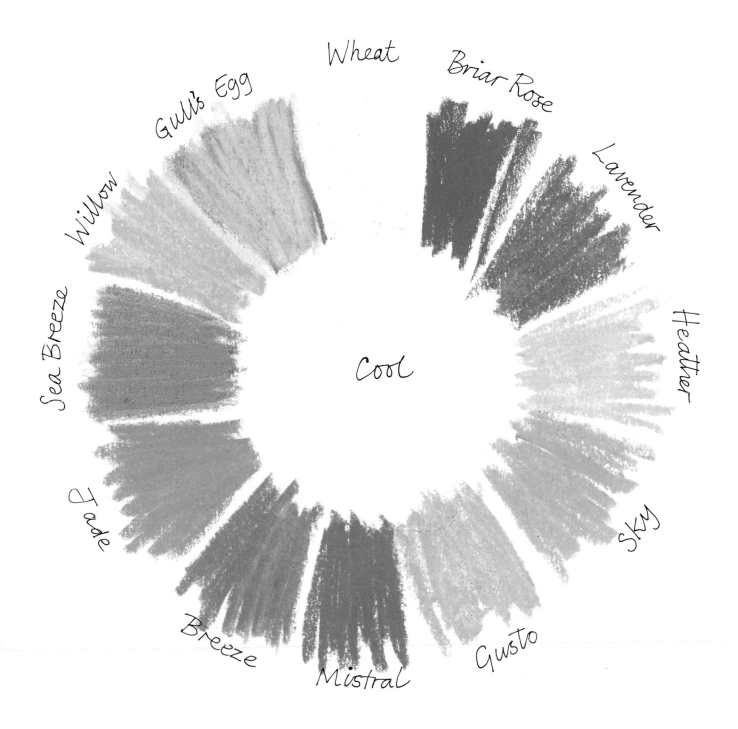

Wheat

Briar Rose

Gull's Egg

Lavender

Willow

Heather

Sea Breeze

Cool

Sky

Jade

Gusto

Breeze

Mistral

Wind immediately evokes a sense of movement and change, and succesful colour schemes based on the wind palette do the same. This palette can be used anywhere in the home. Wind rooms are relaxed, with an emphasis on flexibility: never boring, they lend themselves to a combination of patterns and plains. They are a dependable choice in any room where you want the atmosphere to be inviting and interesting, without being too dramatic.

The wind palette is soft, welcoming and invigorating. These colours lie midway between the pastels that characterize the air palette and the clarity and depth of the water palette. This gives them a subtlety and at the same time a particularly versatile quality. To make the most of the wind colours, choose a combination of several shades to work together in the same room.

From the warm side of the palette, create a colour scheme using Sirocco, Shadow and Clover or, if working with the cool colours, try using Sky and Heather together.

Colour scheming with wind colours is a joy as, subtle as they may appear, they also possess a quiet gaiety that is easy on the eye and restful to live with, but at the same time encourages experimentation. With this palette you can be quite adventurous in your choice of patterns and colours since it can withstand quite bold and highly patterned designs, combined with richly coloured rugs and pictures. Remember too that you can use the softer natural colours as a base or as accents to complete your colour scheme. Wind colours work well in rooms of any aspect and add definition to small spaces. A combination of them reinforces the sense of movement.

LEFT The division between indoors and out is reduced by choosing cool greens that pick up the colours of the foliage outside the bathroom of this suburban home.

RIGHT The warm yellows of the wind palette provide a strong background colour for a collection of prints. The brass bedstead enriches the effect of the yellow paintwork, while the floral pattern of the counterpane gives the room a fresh, summery atmosphere.

THE WATER PALETTE

Waterfalls, rivers, oceans, showers and snowfall – water is the element that flows through and around, constantly changing its form. But whatever form it comes in, water is like an empty container for light, making it an element whose hallmark is clarity.

Whether warm or cool, the colours of the water palette all share this quality of clarity and depth. They have a crispness that makes you want to use them in a way that reflects an uncluttered, happy home. The water colours combine beautifully with the stark simplicity of Pearl and Snowflake in the natural palette, especially in bathrooms and kitchens. Water colours have a vividness and energy that can make for effective colour schemes based on using only one or two colours alongside each other.

From the cool side of the palette Waterfall, Fountain and Ultramarine make great bathroom colours. If using the warm category, try coordinating Jasper, Periwinkle and Spa, for example, to establish a successful colour scheme in a living room.

If you are tempted to focus on one particular colour from the water palette in order to maximize its impact, remember that you can increase the effect by using coordinating tones of the same colour as accents. For example, use Mallard as a main room colour, with Waterfall and Serpentine as the accent colours. Small details like painting a recess or the woodwork in a coordinating or a contrasting colour will give your colour scheme a touch of flair and individuality.

LEFT Cool, minty greens enliven the walls of this dining room and provide an assertive background for the display of plates and prints, as well as contrasting with the dark wood of the antique cabinet.

RIGHT The division of this wall space into large expanses of warm blue and yellow gives this bathroom a note of understated elegance, an effect which is increased by the use of spongeing as a paint effect.

THE
FIRE
PALETTE

With fire, we come to an element that is bright and vibrant with energy. We often associate fire with destruction, but fire has its quiet aspects too. Think of the glowing embers of a campfire, the gentle warmth of summer evening sun, the blue-white flicker of candlelight. Here is fire that warms and brightens its surroundings.

Having said this, it is definitely the case that fire colours in decorating can be hot to handle! More than the other palettes, fire colours must be used carefully and in moderation in order not to overpower the room. However, they can look stunning used as a single colour over a large surface area. Colours such as Sunshine and Tourmaline from the warm palette make wonderfully dramatic wall colours. The Ruby, Sapphire and Emerald cool colours make excellent choices for large sofas, curtains and Roman blinds.

Fire colours work beautifully on fabrics that have a natural shine, such as silk and chintz. They can be offset by bold, contemporary floral designs and by intricately patterned carpets and rugs. The fire palette also works well in children's rooms. If you want to make an impact in your home and are drawn to the fire palette, start with a signature colour, combined perhaps with a neutral white, and build up the colour scheme once you see the effect the main colour has in the room.

LEFT The rich fiery reds of the heavy silk curtains combine with the carpet colours to create a bright and dramatic warm colour scheme in this sitting room.

RIGHT Cool, pure bright cobalt walls give a dramatic feel to this compact town kitchen, in keeping with its modern, uncluttered style.

THE
EARTH
PALETTE

THE EARTH PALETTE

The earth palette divides into warm and cool base colours.
Once you have completed the questionnaire on pages 124-5,
and have discovered if you are essentially warm- or cool-
based, use the appropriate wheel to select your colours.
These can then be used in decorating or furnishing your
room, either on their own or in combination with colours
from the warm or cool side of the other palettes.

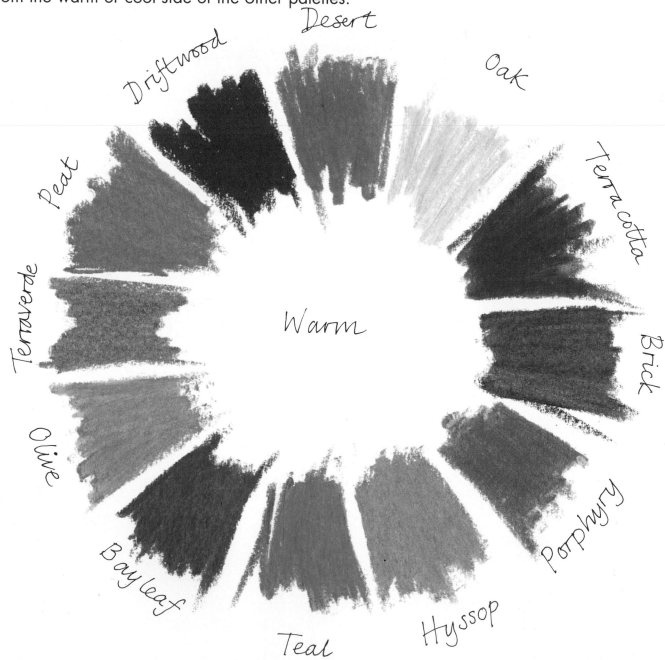

Desert

Driftwood

Oak

Peat

Terracotta

Terraverde

Warm

Brick

Olive

Porphyry

Bayleaf

Teal

Hyssop

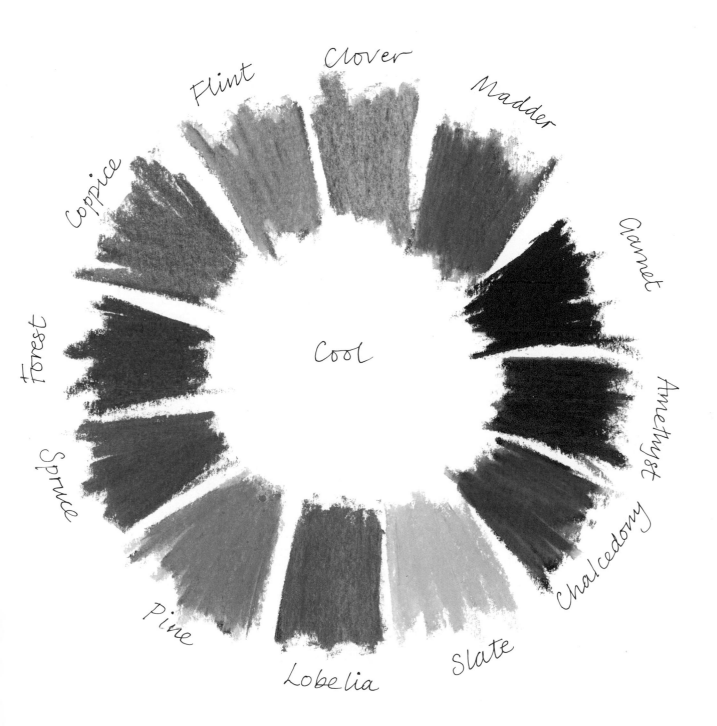

Imagine yourself standing on a green carpet, with a yellow wall on your right and a floral wall on your left. Of course, you are not in a room at all, you are in the countryside, with corn ripening on the hill to your right, and a garden on your left. The colours of the earth palette echo the colours of the natural world and while the colours of each season may change, the background colours – the colours of the earth – are always present.

The earth palette is both rich and dark, muted and sombre. These colours lend themselves most naturally to downstairs rooms, where you want an atmosphere of solid well-being, stability and purpose. They make excellent colours for living rooms, studies, and dining rooms, not forgetting hallways and corridors. For a dining room, consider using Terracotta or Terraverde from the warm palette; Spruce or Garnet from the cool category. If your rooms receive little natural light, use the richness of the earth palette to enhance them.

The colours of the earth palette work well with dark wood furniture. Mahogany, oak and walnut are particularly effective. Ethnic wooden furnishings from Africa and the Far East are set off to good effect by earth colours, as are large items of wooden furniture such as dining room tables and four-poster beds.

LEFT The bath is the most important object in any bathroom. Here, its significance is given extra visual emphasis by the contrast between the fiery orange paintwork of the main room and the stark ivory tiles on the walls around the bath. Orange is a difficult colour to work with on this scale: here, its possibilities are exploited to the full by loose dragging. Black and white fittings add a final dramatic flourish.

RIGHT Cool, earthy ochres and dark woodwork accentuate the rustic charm of an unusual oval window in a kitchen.

THE
MINERAL
PALETTE

LIVING WITH COLOUR

EVERY BUILDING HAS ITS OWN CHARACTER. WHEN YOU BUY A NEW PROPERTY, OR TAKE A STEP BACK FROM YOUR CURRENT HOME AND CONSIDER CHANGING IT, YOU ARE GIVING YOURSELF THE OPPORTUNITY TO DEVELOP THAT CHARACTER IN A WAY THAT WILL SUIT YOUR OWN REQUIREMENTS. THE NATURAL FEATURES OF A HOME ARE ENHANCED WHEN IT IS DECORATED WITH SENSITIVITY AND CONFIDENCE, GIVING THE PERSONALITY AND TASTE OF THE OWNER ITS FULLEST EXPRESSION. THE MANY EXAMPLES IN THIS SECTION WILL SHOW YOU THE VARIED EFFECTS THAT CAN BE CREATED BY DIFFERENT COLOUR PALETTES AND WILL HELP YOU TO SEE WHAT YOU MIGHT ACHIEVE WITH YOUR OWN COLOUR PALETTES.

INTRODUCTION

The inherent character of any home is its primary asset, regardless of scale, age or location. That character may have been concealed for decades or centuries due to clumsy or inappropriate renovation; poor use of available materials; and, more often than not, an unimaginative use of colour.

BELOW The rustic stonework and curved ceiling of this sitting room are left to speak for themselves with the simplest white paint treatment. This natural look continues with the dark-stained boards of the floor and the wooden furnishings. On the sofa, richly patterned reds, browns and ochres from the earth palette introduce a new and appropriately rustic texture. Above the sofa, a carefully placed mirror reflects and emphasizes the curve of the ceiling.

But if you have ever looked for a new property, either to rent or to buy, you will recognize the feeling that comes when you find somewhere that, with a new coat of paint here and some carpentry work there, has the potential to be transformed in a way that will reflect your personal taste and style. When you select a new property, the chances are that whatever its condition, you are choosing this place because you can sense that by making a few – or perhaps more than a few – critical changes, you can create somewhere you will be happy to have as your home.

The room-by-room analysis in this chapter is intended to help you to identify the chief characteristics of your home, and to develop your own colour schemes so as to create a living space which is in keeping with your taste and lifestyle. Before looking at rooms on an individual basis, however, it is important that you consider your home as a whole. Even if you plan, in the first instance, to decorate only one room, you need to be aware of how your colour scheme in that space will influence, and be influenced by, the spaces around it.

One of the easiest mistakes an inexperienced decorator can make is to create several different colour schemes in neighbouring rooms, without taking into account the way in which the different colours will affect each other, and the people who spend time in them. Colour always makes an impact. This is true even of the most neutral surroundings. The colours used to decorate a space have an immediate psychological influence on anyone using that space. There may be walls, doors and even stairwells between them, but a succession of rooms in which completely different colour palettes have been used will have an unsettling and disjointed effect.

This is not to say that you should not feel free to experiment with colour – a house that is decorated in a monotone way, unless it is designed with particular flair, can feel lifeless and dreary – but before you start decorating even a small room, take into account how your plans will relate to the rest of the house.

COLOUR AND LIGHT

If you can, give yourself time. Because of the inseparability of colour and light, the colours you choose for a room will change according to the time of year, not only because there is more sunlight in the summer months, but also because the quality of light thrown by the sun at different times of year can alter the character of a room quite drastically. This is particularly true of west-facing rooms, where the windows will be dark by late afternoon in winter but flooded by sunshine well into the evening during the summer months. The same differences apply to the morning light in east-facing rooms, though they will probably be less relevant, unless you are a very early riser. North- and south-facing rooms will not change to the same extent at different times of year, but you will need to consider whether the natural light is going to be blocked by nearby buildings or by overhanging trees, especially when the sun is low in winter.

Pay attention to detail when you are planning a colour scheme. Imagine the room like a jigsaw puzzle where all the pieces have to fit together. It is surprising how easily a well coordinated room can be thrown out of balance. A picture frame of the wrong colour can ruin the appearance of an otherwise harmonious colour scheme. So can a badly placed lamp, or an inappropriate lampshade – red lampshades, for example, throw a pink cast unless they have a white or ivory lining. Even a vase of flowers can spoil a room if the colours are not in keeping with their surroundings.

Last but not least, enjoy yourself. Experiment. When you are looking for inspiration, do not be afraid to ask for as many samples as you like. Daub test pots of paint on the wall and pin up wallpaper and fabric samples alongside. Visit the room off and on over a period of time, noting the difference in the colour samples between daylight and artificial light. Be adventurous. Remember that once you have decided on your colour palette, you have a completely sound base from which to transform your home. You don't need to make expensive mistakes, and if you make the occasional cheap one, you should regard it as part of a natural learning process, not as a sign that you don't know what you are doing.

Successful colour scheming turns around a few elementary rules. Once you have mastered them, the floor, the ceiling and everything in between are yours.

DESIGNING YOUR HOME

Even if they are the same size and shape and built out of the same materials, no two houses have ever been alike, for the simple reason that they cannot both share the same plot of ground – and the setting of a house plays a major part in its character. So your starting point in colour scheming your home is to consider its setting.

THE HOUSE AS A UNIT

Be aware of the expectations your house awakens in you as you approach it, then consider how you can best realize those expectations. Are there any features outside the house that you want to continue to develop inside it? For example, if your home is in a rural setting, is this a theme you want to continue indoors? If you live in a city, are there historical aspects of the city as a whole, and your neighbourhood in particular, that you would like to echo inside? Or do you want to achieve a complete change of environment as you step across the threshold?

A SIGNATURE COLOUR

Colour can extend walls, raise and lower ceilings, eliminate corners. It can make the same space airy or womblike; formal or intimate; stimulating or peaceful. To achieve a sense of continuity and openness, use the same colour for the walls and carpets of successive rooms. To achieve a sense of distance and separation, choose contrasting colours. You may like to combine these options in different areas of your home. For example, you may want your living room and hall to connect visually, and then to have a contrast between the living room and the kitchen.

LEFT The chief architectural features of this bedroom are the wooden panelled ceiling, the handsome fireplace and the windows on either side. This room receives plenty of natural light, a feature which the owner has developed by choosing pale whites and ivories to establish the signature colour. Additional interest is achieved by the use of contrasting textures on the carpet, armchairs and curtains, and by introducing dark colour accents with the bed frame, curtain poles, mirror frame, candlesticks, lampstand and chair.

ABOVE In this kitchen earth colours are combined with accents from the water palette. Handsome, blue-green cupboards provide the storage space and the foreground colour. A pale wooden work surface divides the upper and lower units and at the same time picks up the mellow apricot-pink of the walls. This warm base colour in turn offsets the display of blue and white china.

However you plan your overall scheme, establish a signature colour. One of the simplest ways of establishing this connection is by having the same floor surface running throughout the house. But this is not the only way of creating a sense of unity – you may choose to have the colour of the wall paint in your entrance hall echoed in one of the colours in a patterned living room carpet, for example, or in the curtains of a bedroom. When you select a signature colour and make sure it is used, however minimally, as a connecting thread running through your house, your overall colour scheme will cohere in a way that is both visually and psychologically satisfying.

When a house has distinctive features, it is better to emphasize than to ignore them. If you try to play them down, you run the risk of the house disappearing into its own borders. Strong features call for strong definition. If you house has architectural features such as exposed beams, unusually proportioned rooms, interesting alcoves or detailed woodwork, play up the benefits of these features. With wood panelling, echo the feature of the panels by painting recessed surfaces darker than relief ones. Paint the interiors of cupboards and the backs of shelving a shade darker than the walls to emphasize their depth.

Although it sounds too obvious to require attention, be aware of who, besides yourself, your home is intended for. If you have a partner whose taste does not entirely accord with your own, resolve your differences if you can by allocating him or her one room and giving yourself another. Avoid the kind of compromise by which one person chooses the carpet and the other the wallpaper. If you have small children, you will need to pay attention to the wear and tear factor and choose flooring and wall treatments that will withstand the thundering of small feet and the patina of sticky fingers. And if you share a house with teenagers, make sure you leave them enough space for their own particular kind of self-expression.

Be conscious of your budget as you work out your colour scheme. A few pots of paint can go further in transforming a home than a week's worth of carpentry. Give yourself time to be a sleuth and check out different manufacturers' prices. Don't be afraid to negotiate a discount, especially if you are buying large quantities of fabric or flooring. Besides considering the expense of the materials themselves, consider the cost in time that will be devoted to decorating. Decide too just how much time you have to spend in maintaining your home. For example, if you like the idea of filling a window frame with rows of coloured glass vases that will sparkle like gems in the light, consider how often they will have to be cleaned. Some colours show the dirt much more easily than others – avoid black tiles in the bathroom and kitchen if you want to have a low-maintenance home.

PLANNING AHEAD

First work out your priorities. If you need to do some rewiring to achieve the lighting effects you want, think ahead and make sure the electrical work is carried out before you start decorating. Check for damp and dry rot too and ensure that window and door frames and skirting boards are in good condition before you strip and repaint them. It is more economical, in the long run, to attend to these basic areas of maintenance before you embark on a decorating programme.

If you are the kind of person who enjoys variety and likes to alter your surroundings on quite a regular basis, introduce elements that can be inexpensively altered for a different effect. Rugs, lampshades, cushions and wool throws in a sitting room; towels and soaps in a bathroom; new biscuit tins, place mats and chair covers in a kitchen can all ring colour changes with minimal financial outlay.

THE THREE COLOUR KEYS

All the colours contained within a living space play a part in creating the character of that space. But, as a basic rule, the colours in a room can be subdivided into the following three areas:

Base colours
Foreground colours
Colour accents

Each of these colour keys has an essential role. And the relationship in both colour and tone between the different colour keys is as important as the contribution made by them individually.

Base colours All shades of colour have a base 'note'. With primary colours, that note is inseparable from the colour itself – primary red does not have any other colour added to it, nor does primary blue or yellow. However, the majority of paints, wallpapers and furnishing fabrics on the market are made out of secondary or tertiary colours, in an almost infinite variety of tints and shades. The base note of a tertiary colour can differ from the 'apparent' surface colour. For example, a light beige with a blue base will alter in its effect from a light beige with a yellow base.

As discussed in the first chapter, all colours have either a warm base or a cool base. When choosing your colours, you need, first, to be clear about which you are selecting. The difference between a warm green and a cool green may appear to be slight on a paint chart or a fabric sample, but when that colour is used across an extensive surface in a room, the base colour in the paint will have a significant influence on the result. Your base colour is not only the base note of the paint, wallpaper or fabric which you have

chosen, it is also the basis of your overall colour scheme. In some cases the base colour of a room is already apparent. If, for example, you have a wooden floor that you do not wish to cover, that will establish the base colour for the room and you need to choose a wall colour that complements the wood.

The base colours of any space are the colours that occupy the widest areas – usually the walls, the floor and the ceiling. Because the impact of a colour increases in direct proportion to the expanse it covers, the quality of the base colour has an overriding influence on the character of a room.

Foreground colours Foreground colours are the colours that dominate in the furnishings of a room. They can include the colours in sofas, tables, chairs, beds, mantelpieces, alcoves and shelving, floor rugs, curtains and blinds. Foreground colours need to harmonize with the

base colours, which means that your base colour needs to be either present or suggested in your foreground colours. The only exception to this is if you are intentionally creating a dramatic effect, which is achieved by combining strongly contrasting base and foreground colours.

If your foreground colours are mixed, as in a multi-coloured sofa or a patterned set of curtains, you have the opportunity to select a base colour that will emphasize one of the colours in your furnishing scheme. For example, a patterned curtain fabric which contains some pink will look pinker if the walls are painted pink than if they are painted pale grey. Conversely, you may choose to work with more than one base colour, such as deciding on a striped wallpaper. In this case, you may opt to select a foreground colour which strengthens the presence in the room of one or other of the colours used in the design of the wallpaper covering the walls.

ABOVE LEFT The fire palette plays a dominant role as the foreground colour in this sitting room. Strong, geometric patterns on the central rug and in the curtains link these two features and introduce a wide range of colours. The red trim of the chairs accentuates this colour and contrasts strongly both with the dark green fabric and with the pale walls and window frame behind.

ABOVE The textures of both plain and painted wood, paintwork, glazed cups and saucers, eggs, fruit and flowers all play a part in making the colour scheme of this kitchen interesting as well as harmonious.

Colour accents Colour accents are colours that are introduced to enliven the overall colour scheme of a room. Colour accents may be introduced through cushions, stencil patterns, wall friezes and dado rails, skirting boards, piping on soft furnishings, picture and photograph mounts and frames, lamp bases and lampshades, found objects, wall hangings and table settings. Because the interplay between complementary colours is livelier than that between harmonious or matching colours, colour accents are often complementary to the base colour in a room. Thus, red accents will introduce energy and warmth to a green room, while purple accents will glamorize a yellow-based room. However, the neutrals can also perform well as accents – a few charcoal grey accents will introduce sophistication in a yellow colour scheme and soften the impact of a predominantly red room. White as a colour accent can throw into sharper relief many rich and dark shades, while dark brown and black can give definition and strength to pale, off-white colour schemes.

THE INFLUENCE OF TEXTURE

Chintz, linen, calico. Wool, seagrass, slate. Pine, walnut, formica. All of these different textures, and more, contribute to the effect colours have on a room. This is due in part to the varying ways in which light plays off objects of different textures, and partly to the way placing different textures alongside each other has a tactile as well as a visual impact on a room. Combining a wide variety of textures is one of the best ways of bringing interest to a monochrome room decorating scheme. Conversely, combining as few textures as possible can increase the sense of space and introduce a note of restrained elegance to a colour scheme.

Wood When it is unvarnished, wood has a matt surface which will absorb light rather than reflecting it, the effect of this being to create a restful, rustic atmosphere. Unvarnished wood can be a marvellous starting point for a colour scheme – like any natural material, wood contains a myriad of subtly different shades and colours that alter from hour to hour with changes of light.

Because of its shiny surface, varnished wood reflects light. This makes it a stylish and dramatic choice for rooms that will be used for entertaining in the evening. The play of candlelight or electric light on highly varnished wood creates an atmosphere of sparkling elegance, which is emphasized by the contrast between the solidity of the wood and the floating, translucent quality of the light. The interplay between wood and light is further

enhanced by the use of a dark base colour – this applies to both unvarnished and varnished wooden surfaces. The mid-blues make particularly comfortable companions to wood, as do the blue-greens, while the mid-reds create a more energetic mood.

Glass Glass is an excellent way of enhancing light and accentuating colour in a room. Before the advent of electricity, this consideration was a salient factor in the choice of crystal and coloured glass for chandeliers. Glass objects

ABOVE The wooden door of this hall is given special importance by being painted bright red, which sets it off from everything around it and underlines its significance as an entrance.

LEFT Against a stark white background, a rich and subtle combination of tiles from the mineral palette provides the foreground colour in this shower room. Brightly coloured towels are all that is needed to provide colour accents.

are best positioned where they can catch light and extend it – they are wasted in recesses and shadowy corners. All kinds of glass objects – clear, coloured or opaque – will introduce a note of richness and brightness to a room. Clear glass will also pick up the colours around it, while coloured glass can be used as a colour accent that will seem to float against the surfaces behind it. Judiciously placed mirrors are also valuable allies in planning a colour scheme, as they can reflect another room and prepare one for a change of colour in moving to another setting.

DECORATING DOS AND DON'TS

DO

✔ Make structural changes, such as rewiring, reflooring or building shelves, before you start to decorate

✔ Establish a budget

✔ Consider the function of each room in turn, including:
- the time of day it will be used
- how many people are likely to use it at any given time
- the amount of wear and tear it will receive
- the amount of time you can commit to maintaining it
- its location in relation to the rest of the house
- its light sources, both natural and artificial
- storage

✔ Select a signature colour

✔ Be aware that the colours of one room will affect those around it

✔ Note all architectural details

✔ Experiment with sample boards

✔ Take into account the needs and tastes of family or house mates

DON'T

✘ Buy the first fabric or paint you like without researching the market

✘ Mix and match colours before you have compared them as samples

✘ Make guesses: measure, compare and consider before you buy

✘ Be impractical – you will probably regret a white carpet

✘ Ignore details

✘ Hurry – introduce your new colour elements stage by stage

✘ Take short cuts

✘ Combine colours from different palettes unless you are intentionally creating a specific effect

✘ Use lots of black and purple

✘ Paint over valuable wooden furniture. Sell the piece and buy cheaper wood if you want to use paint

MAKING A SAMPLE BOARD

Professional interior designers use sample boards as a way of experimenting with possible combinations of colour, texture and style. The sample board enables you to see in miniature how well different colours, fabrics and patterns look alongside each other. It also gives you a cheap, easy and enjoyable way of adding and subtracting different elements to your room design. To swap one fabric for another on a sample board will cost you next to nothing; to have another complete set of curtains made because your first choice did not work out is not only expensive, it also undermines your confidence and stops you giving your sense of colour its fullest expression.

So, make the preparation of sample boards a priority for every room you plan to decorate. Photocopy the checklist on this page as many times as you need and take it with you when you go shopping. Then follow the four easy steps listed opposite. Even if you know it will take you two or three years to buy everything you want in your new room, do not be afraid to include all the items on the sample board. The clearer your vision is at the start, the more complete your room will look at the finish. And simply by arranging and rearranging the ingredients of the sample board, you will learn more about colour, and also about your own stylistic

preferences, than you will by searching through sample after sample in a soft furnishings shop.

CHECKLIST

SIZE
○ How big is your room?
○ width.......................
○ length.......................
○ height.......................

COLOUR
○ Which existing colours do you wish to retain? Which new colours do you wish to introduce?
- floor
- ceiling
- carpet/rug
- woodwork
- curtains
- soft furnishings
- walls
- furniture
- accessories
- pictures
- lampshades and stands

LIGHT
○ How much natural light does the room receive, and at what time of day?
○ What kind of artificial light do you wish to use?
- overhead
- standard lamps
- uplighters
- candles

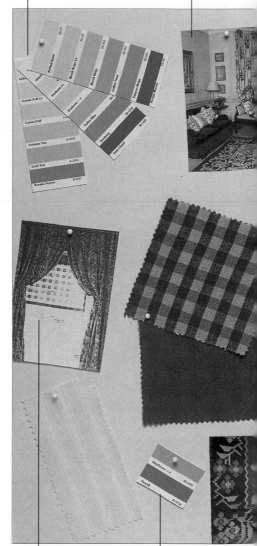

Use different shades of a colour via 'colourize' paint charts – build up your colour palette with different cards

A photograph of a room your last home acts a reminder the furnish you have.

Use photographs from magazines to illustrate different curtain styles.

Individual paint colours for specific projects

Photographs of the room as it is now act as a reminder of what has to be done and what is in the room.

Have a large sample of the main fabric to use as a base for the other items.

Take photographs of rugs to help you colour-coordinate fabrics and other furnishings.

Build up a collection of coordinating fabrics that can be used for cushions and general colour accents.

Try out a large sample of fabric to see if the scale suits the piece of furniture.

STEP 1

Buy a piece of foam board 40cm x 60cm (16 x 24in) and a pack of thumb tacks at your local art supplier. Assemble on the board samples of all the items in the room, such as furnishing fabric, which you wish to keep as they are. Take photographs of any large items such rugs, lamps, pictures or main pieces of furniture so these can be included on the sample board in some way.

STEP 2

Add samples, such as pieces of carpet or paint manufacturer's colour charts, for each of the base colours you are considering.

STEP 3

Now add samples of, for example, curtain or upholstery fabric for all the foreground colours you are considering using.

STEP 4

Finally, add samples of coordinating colours and colour accents, in the form of fabric for cushion-covers or throws, tablecloths or lampshades.

Do not regard each of these stages as rigid. The purpose of making a sample board is to enable you to go to and fro, adding and subtracting different base, foreground and accent colours, to get a sense of how the room will work as a unit once it is finished. Move the different samples around on the board so that you can see how the atmosphere of your room may change, depending on which colours are placed alongside each other. With the sample board in the room you intend to decorate, see how the colours you have selected change at different times of day.

THE ENTRANCE HALL

Your entrance hall gives you your first opportunity to say ' this is who I am'. You may want to make this statement discreet, playful or dramatic.

Whatever your inclination, the way in which you decorate the entrance hall will be the first indication to visitors of your taste and lifestyle and the way in which you are likely to have planned the rest of your home. Your entrance hall will show, among other things, how seriously you take yourself; how strong your sense of colour is; how effectively you are able to introduce yourself to others. Even when they amount to a space no larger than a corridor, entrances speak – and because they have the first say, it is worth taking them seriously.

THE FRONT DOOR

The entrance hall starts with the front door, and the walls on either side of it. To what extent do you want the characteristics that lie outside your home to be extended indoors? If you are lucky enough to live in a beautiful rural location, you may opt to emphasize the character of the local materials by painting the walls of the entrance hall in a hue that echoes that of the outer stonework, or the colours of the countryside. Similarly, if you have a brick house, you may wish to carry indoors the natural warmth that much brickwork contains. On the other hand, if you feel that the exterior of your home lacks character, or if you want to introduce a different character to that which is outside, here is the place to establish your personal identity.

PROPORTIONS AND WAYS WITH WALL SPACE

Consider the proportions of the space you have to work with. If your hall is tall and narrow, and you want to break up the walls, it is worth considering a dado rail, with the area below the rail painted a solid colour and the area above wallpapered or painted a lighter shade. As well as

RIGHT The colour of natural wood combines with a warm green from the earth palette in this spacious hallway – a wise choice in a space that receives little natural light.

○ The tiled floor coordinates with the warm wood of the staircase and doorway.

○ Wooden bookshelves around the far door frame make a distinctive feature out of a wall area that would otherwise be inconspicuous.

○ The wood and fabric of the director's chair pick up the two main colours of the room.

○ The theme of wood is continued in the coat rail, which also makes good use of what would otherwise be wasted space.

○ Four overhead spotlights focus discreetly but effectively on the centre of the room.

RIGHT Three harmonizing paint colours from the water palette bring elegance as well as light to this simple stairwell. Note that the back of the alcove on the left is painted the same soft mauve as the stairwell, accentuating the light green wall and taking the eye upstairs. The airy wall colours are beautifully offset by the golden sheen of the varnished wooden floor.

FAR RIGHT Here the dado rail gives architectural balance to a narrow, panelled hallway, set off by the unusual random mix of different coloured floor tiles.

being an effective way of dividing vertical space, a dado rail also gives you the opportunity to use a practical colour for the lower wall surfaces, which are likely to receive the most wear and tear. Alternatively, you may have a hallway which is large enough to be treated as a reception room. In very old houses, halls were often multi-functional, containing a large fireplace as a focal point and intended to be used both for relaxation and eating. Large entrance halls are also a characteristic of many Georgian and Edwardian houses. If your entrance hall offers the kind of space that can accommodate a sitting area, a desk by a window or a child's rocking horse, you will be able to plan your colour scheme around these objects and create an ambience which tempts the visitor to stop and linger for a while.

Do not be deceived into thinking that a narrow entrance hall, with space for no more than a hat stand, has to be boring. As advertisers know well, people enjoy being diverted as they move from one place to another – witness the number of advertisements on roadsides and in underground stations. An entrance hall can make a most effective picture gallery, even if space is at a premium. You do not need to be an art connoisseur, or to spend a lot of money, to hang a row of pictures, prints or photographs in your hallway.

HANGING PICTURES

If you do choose to hang pictures in an entrance hall, you need to be conscious of lighting. It is no use having a fascinating arrangement of prints if no-one can see them properly. If you choose overhead lighting, you need to make sure that the fittings you choose throw sufficient light to do justice to all of your picture collection. You may also consider having a discreet tube of light running below a picture rail, or a pair of strategically placed uplighters. Many entrance halls, particularly in apartments and town houses, do not have a source of natural light from windows so it is worth taking time and trouble over lighting this part of your home well. Nothing is less inviting than stepping into a poorly lit entrance hall.

Bear in mind that many pictures are enhanced by being hung against a dark colour. Black and white prints can look dramatic against deep blues, greens and reds, as can

old family photographs. Yellow makes a better background for works of art that contain a lot of colour – its brightness can overpower sepia or black-and-white images.

Mounts play an important part in the overall effect of a display of pictures. It may seem to be a small detail, but pictures that have an ivory mount will look different from those with a cream or a light blue mount. Similarly, gilt frames will introduce a different accent to plain wood or lacquer frames. Pictures can also be decorated with ribbons and bows. Pay attention not only to the images you choose, but the way in which you mount, frame and hang them.

SPECIAL PAINT EFFECTS

If you prefer to make the walls a feature in their own right, you might consider using a patterned wallpaper, or a special paint effect such as ashlar. Because the entrance hall is the crossover place between the outer and inner worlds, it is an ideal space in which to paint imitation brickwork or stonework. A hallway can also be enhanced by having a stencilled frieze or a stencilled dado rail.

FLOORING

Flooring is of primary importance in entrance halls. This is the place where mud, rain and slush will be brought inside during wintery weather, where umbrellas will drip on the floor and where rain will run from overcoats. One way to remind people that they are no longer outside is to devote several feet of your entrance hall to coarse matting which is specifically intended for vigorous shoe and boot-rubbing. If you do not have the space or the inclination for this, make sure that you have a decent doormat and that the flooring of the rest of the entrance hall is hard-wearing, easy to clean and of a shade that does not make every speck of dirt shine out like a beacon.

CONNECTING ROOMS WITH COLOUR

More often than not, entrance halls connect to several rooms, so however you decorate the hallway, you need to ensure a smooth transition from this part of the home to the rooms that lead off it. You don't need to repeat every colour in your hall in all of the neighbouring rooms, but you should not change absolutely everything either. As discussed earlier in this section, establish your signature colour and pick it up again, either as a base or a fore-ground colour, in the adjacent living spaces.

STAIRWELLS

If you are laying a new carpet on the stairs, you can choose whether to run the carpet right across the stair width or leave a border of white or natural woodwork on either side of the carpet. In a house with one or more upper landings, you can introduce a subtle change of atmosphere on each floor. For example, you may paint the walls of your ground floor in a warm off-white, then enrich this on the first floor with a warm cream and brighten it on the sec-ond floor with a stronger yellow. Or you may select a dark, assertive green on the ground floor, changing to a pat-terned paper on the first floor in which the same green is a secondary colour, and taking the primary colour of the wallpaper as your theme for the second floor. Whatever you decide, aim to achieve an effect which makes your entrance hall interesting in its own right and a space which invites the visitor to explore further.

Many town houses have narrow hallways which can feel tunnel-like and which have nowhere to place a piece of furniture. By introducing a dado rail, placing a shelf above the radiator and continuing the dado moulding around the shelf, you create a useful display and storage space while maintaining a unified look. Adding a mirror above the dado rail gives a feeling of width and space and sets off the display of prints to advantage.

YOU WILL NEED:

❍ Length of wooden dado moulding, approximately 5cm (2in) deep, to go round the mirror and the shelf

❍ Length of timber for wooden shelf, approximately 17cm (7in) deep and 1.5cm (⅝in) thick. For the length, measure that of the radiator itself and add 20-30cm (8-12in) to allow space on either side to fix brackets

❍ A pair of shelf brackets and 50mm (2in) screws for fixing

❍ Spirit level

❍ Mirror glass cut to size and 4 flat mirror screws for fixing

❍ Narrow wooden beading as long as the width of the mirror

CREATING SPACE IN A NARROW HALL

1. Buy the mirror glass with a hole drilled at each corner and screw it to the wall, centred above the radiator, using the flat screws. Fix the dado rail along the hall walls, stopping 10-15cm (4-6in) from the radiator, at each side.

2. Screw the first bracket in position, using a wall plug in a solid wall, then use a shelf and spirit level to position the second bracket and fix it in the same way.

3. Place the shelf in position above the radiator, using a spirit level to align the ends before fixing them securely to the brackets. Continue the dado moulding around the shelf, mitring the corners; use lost-head nails to fix it in place. Fix dado moulding around three sides of the mirror, using wood glue. Finish by applying the narrow wooden beading to cover the base of the mirror.

CAROLYN'S TIPS

❝ By painting the mirror frame and dado rail a pale colour, you will enhance the feeling of space and light in the hall. ❞

❝ To lower a high ceiling, paint the dado rail a darker colour. ❞

❝ Create colour accents by painting the mirror frame in a contrasting colour. ❞

THE LIVING ROOM

In any home the living room calls for special attention since it is the room in which the family will spend time together and visitors will be entertained.

Planning a colour scheme for a living room means creating a space in which everyone can quickly feel at their ease and ready to socialize. At their worst, living rooms are cold and inhospitable, making it difficult to relax. At their best, they are warm, inviting and so comfortable that you find it difficult to leave them.

COLOUR AND COMFORT

Colour and comfort are key factors in the creation of a successful living room. These two themes come together in the choices you make for the upholstery of your armchairs and sofas, since these are likely to make up the most dominant foreground colours in the room. Solid colours are often a popular choice, and if you follow this route you can introduce a variety of patterns and textures with scatter cushions and wool throws. Alternatively, you may opt to reverse this process and choose a multicoloured upholstery fabric, highlighting a particular colour within it by using plain cushions.

Colour and comfort are also the key themes in creating a living room that is as welcoming to one person as it is to many. For most of us, the living room is a multi-functional space. You will probably want to feel as settled in it when you are alone as you do when you are hosting a party or having your sister and her children to tea. It is horrible to sit in a room and feel you are surrounded by empty spaces. A simple way of resolving this problem is by varying the upholstery you choose for different sofas and armchairs. Not only does this break up the space visually, it also has the psychological benefit of separating different items of furniture so that their presence is not overbearing to the solitary occupant.

RIGHT Powerful reds from the mineral palette give an inviting and almost oriental character to this sitting room.

❍ The bold, star-patterned wallpaper is beautifully offset by the blue marbled paintwork below the dado rail.

❍ Two wall bracket lights balance the gold-framed Indian cushion covers which are treated as pictures, while the lamps on either side of the sofa create a pleasing contrast of colour and scale.

❍ White-painted woodwork separates the dark colours from each other and lightens the room's overall effect. At the same time it accentuates the contrast between the red wallpaper and sofa and the blue paint below the dado.

❍ The red sofa repeats the signature colour of the room and the richly patterned array of cushions unites all the colours together.

LEFT The exposed wooden beams are a distinctive feature of this country sitting room. The natural theme continues in the carpet and the background colour on the walls and is picked up in all the soft furnishings.

RIGHT Simple base colours from the natural palette provide the perfect foil for a range of decorative items from the earth palette, including the display of pottery and books on the shelves and the magnificent textile on the right-hand wall.

CHOOSING A SIGNATURE COLOUR

As in any room, your choice of signature colour will affect the atmosphere created. If you want a feeling of warmth and intimacy, a rich base colour can be a good choice because the walls will darken during the evening and contrast strongly with the areas of light in the room. This atmosphere can be heightened by choosing a heavy curtain fabric, so that the room feels well-wrapped, especially on cold winter nights.

LIVING WITH RED

Inevitably, reds are popular as living room colours because they have a warming and stimulating effect, making them a distinct asset in a social setting. However, bear in mind that red is a colour which makes objects look larger than they really are. For this reason, red can benefit by being combined with large areas of natural colours, particularly in a small space. If used as background colours on walls, the darker reds need spacious rooms to perform effectively. Used in excess, the drama of red can become darkly claustrophobic. So if you have a red carpet, balance its impact by choosing naturals or light tints for your walls. Conversely, red walls need to be balanced by a more muted floor treatment, though they also look well with the rich patterns of oriental carpets, in which the mix of many deep colours will 'anchor' the red of the walls.

RIGHT Two shades of green, a sage green on the sofa and a blue-green on the walls, establish water as the dominant palette of this sitting room. A rich paisley carpet, heavy wooden furnishings, crowded bookshelves and dark oil paintings create an air of studiousness and privacy.

LIVING WITH YELLOW

Yellows are often chosen for living rooms, particularly in cooler climates. The paler yellows create a sophisticated, elegant atmosphere while the brighter ones can make a large reception room appear more inviting and a small one more luminous and spacious. All the yellows are beautifully complemented by greys, mid-blues and purples, and different shades of yellow can be combined with excellent results – a strong yellow on the walls can be off-set by floral or abstract fabric for curtains and cushions which contain a predominance of creamier yellows and mid-blues. Think of yellow as an accent colour for darker colour schemes.

LIVING WITH BEIGES AND NATURALS

Although it can be dreary when it is used without awareness of its qualities, beige can be an excellent background colour for a living room. Beige is a chameleon, which is strongly affected by its companion colours. When you choose a beige, be aware of its base colour: a pink beige will emphasize reds while a yellow beige will relieve them; a blue beige will complement yellow furnishings while a yellow beige complements green.

The components of many successful colour schemes, naturals can come into their own in living rooms. If you want a room which feels spacious and harmonious, choose a scheme which is predominantly natural, with variety

RIGHT Light-toned natural background colours are punctuated by dark mineral colours in this airy sitting room. The finest of blinds and the white walls take full advantage of the natural light and at the same time create a neutral backdrop for a variety of interesting objects. The handsome marble fireplace is highlighted by hanging a picture above it and placing a hand-crafted vase to one side of the mantelpiece. Black fabric on the chair covers and deep purple cushions provide bold foreground colours and ensure that the overall effect is not too bland.

ABOVE A wide range of carefully chosen colours and textures from the wind palette combine to give this room its charm. The rich reds of the rug make it the centrepiece of the room. This role is emphasised by containing the use of red – repeated only in the tapestry stool. The natural tones are taken up as the signature colour for the hand-painted panelled walls and soft furnishings.

Stylish window treatments do not have to be expensive. The simplest mauve and white gingham has been used for these curtains, their tiny check pattern creating a subtle and pleasing contrast to the plain walls and floral chintzes. Two cushions on the sofa echo the gingham of the curtains, while another two use the same fabric as the cloths on the occasional tables to the left and right of the window. Parchment shades on the lamp cast a warm and mellow light, creating a perfect atmosphere for evening relaxation or entertaining.

introduced through the use of different texture. A few dark accents, particularly dark woods, will enrich a natural colour scheme and create a serene and restful atmosphere.

THE FIREPLACE AS A FOCAL POINT

The focal point of many living rooms is the fireplace. This is often the feature around which the design of the room will turn, particularly if it boasts a distinctive mantelpiece. It may well be the first feature to be seen when entering a room. If your living room has a handsome fireplace, you may regard it as the main source of energy in the room. So the way in which you 'dress' the fireplace makes a signifi-cant statement.

A fireplace can be emphasized by hanging a mirror or a particularly striking picture above it; by running bookshelves or display shelves the full length of the wall on either side of it; and by choosing a fireside rug which complements any colours in the mantelpiece. Other simple and more temporary ways of emphasizing your fireplace include arranging ornaments of a particular type, such as coloured glass, wooden objects or a collection of candlesticks on the mantelpiece; or using the space for a display of miniature books, lacquer boxes or photographs.

LIGHTING

Lighting plays a major part in creating a welcoming atmosphere. Overhead lighting can be severe in living rooms, particularly if the light fitting hangs from the centre of the ceiling. A bright overhead light can easily eclipse other elements in a room, whereas wall brackets, standard lamps and uplighters can be used in combination to emphasize particular features. For a bright atmosphere, combine table lamps with wall lighting, then turn the wall lights down to create a more intimate and informal ambience.

RINGING THE CHANGES

Above all, living rooms are to be enjoyed all year round. Once you have established your colour scheme and installed your main furniture, you are free to experiment – with lighting, with flowers, with rugs, with pictures, with cushions, with shelving. You will be surprised by how many simple ways there are of changing and enhancing the mood of the room according to the season.

CREATE AN INSTANT LIBRARY

What was once a fireplace has been skilfully converted into useful storage space with a trompe l'oeil bookshelf above. A mixture of shades from the wind palette have been combined to make the bookcovers, creating a distinctive feature out of an awkward space.

YOU WILL NEED:

○ Wooden dowelling in three different widths, 1–4cm (½in–1½in) wide, to imitate book spines (offcuts can often be bought more cheaply)

○ Wooden battens 1.5cm x 2cm (⅜in–⅝in) wide to make the fake shelves

○ Wooden dado moulding to surround the bookcase

○ Wood glue

○ Oil-based matt paint in appropriate colours for the shelf fronts, mouldings, background and book spines.

1. Mark out the 'bookcase' area, using a plumb line, steel rule and a pencil, and paint it dark grey or another dark colour. Mark straight horizontal lines on the wall, approximately 25cm (10in) apart, using the steel rule and pencil, then glue the fake shelves in place, leaving space between them for the book spines. Apply the dado moulding around the outside edge, using wood glue. Paint the shelf fronts and dado moulding to match the other woodwork in the room.

2. Cut the wooden dowelling into lengths approximately 23–25cm (9–10in) long, varying them slightly, to make the book spines, and paint them in different colours. Leave to dry. Stick the wooden strips in place, using wood glue. Vary their sizes, colours and positions, to give the random effect of books stored in a bookcase.

CAROLYN'S TIPS

❝ By varying the length and widths of the wooden dowelling, you will create a more realistic 'library' effect. It is a good idea to place some at a slight angle to imitate the appearance of real books leaning against others on a shelf. I have made the lengths of dowelling on the top shelf consistently shorter (approximately 18cm/7in) to give the effect of row of puperback books. ❞

❝ I have painted the book spines a mixture of shades from the wind palette to make an original and eye-catching feature out of what was formerly an awkward space. ❞

INSPIRATION: You can if you wish write witty book titles on the wooden spines.

THE DINING ROOM

Eating together, however informally, is one of the few rituals still practised on a daily basis in households the world over.

In a dining room, the central grouping of a table and chairs at which people will come together to share meals instantly creates an air of formality. Whether the meal is a light brunch, a children's tea or an elaborate dinner party, there is a quality of order, discipline and definition about a table that has been carefully laid for a meal – and the challenge to the interior designer is to bring warmth and character to this setting.

Luckily, this challenge contains its own opportunities. The very fact that dining rooms are used at varying times of day for different types of meal provides scope for creating a room which changes according to the occasion. You may want to reserve your dining room for entertaining only, but if you want a space where you can also spread out your sewing things on the table, let your children sit and do their homework, serve breakfast for six or supper for two, you need to create a setting which is both welcoming and versatile.

THE TABLE AS A FOCAL POINT

The focal point of any dining room is the table and here you can ring the changes cheaply and simply for different occasions. A bright, vinyl-coated tablecloth will protect your tabletop against the activities of pre-school children; crisp white damask, still popular after hundreds of years, is hard to beat for a formal lunch or dinner party, while gingham, paisley and floral tablecloths make excellent backdrops for informal lunches and family meals. You may like to create a layered look by combining a plain, floor-length tablecloth with a shorter, patterned one laid on top of it. This looks particularly effective with round tables, and is an economical way of creating a stylish look without needing to invest in a high-quality table. You can also introduce different colours through tablemats, napkins,

RIGHT A wide range of colours from the earth palette have been brought together in this unusual dining room. The creator of the room has made the most of every inch of space, using images of fruit that make it mouth-watering simply to cross the threshold. This is everything that a dining room should be.

❍ Dark, polished floorboards are left bare, anchoring the plain wooden table and matching benches.

❍ A single curtain of heavy, richly patterned fabric hangs in an extravagant swag, at the same time admitting more light from outside than would be allowed by a pair of curtains. The curtain is hung with an almost theatrical precision, setting the stage for drinks and coffee in the garden beyond.

❍ Warm yellow walls create a fresh, inviting atmosphere and offset a rich range of prints, each displaying a different fruit.

❍ On the table, glassware sparkles in the light, a theme that is discreetly echoed in the lamps on either side of the French windows. Black lampshades both contain and enhance their separate pools of light.

THE KITCHEN

Even in an era of prepared supermarket meals, the kitchen remains the most functional of rooms. It can also be one of the most magnetic.

Who has not been drawn towards the kitchen by the smell of chicken roasting, stews simmering, bread baking or coffee brewing? Kitchens have to do with smell as much as with sight, and this makes the art of creating a successful kitchen more subtle than it may at first appear. Creating a welcoming kitchen relies on choosing colours which will not compete with the invisible centre of the room – the meal that is hidden in the oven, or simmering on top of the stove.

WHITE AS A KITCHEN COLOUR

White is an obvious choice for kitchens. It also has the advantage of reflecting light, an important consideration in a place where food is being prepared. However, white used in excess can begin to look clinical and stark, particularly in a large kitchen, or one that does not benefit from much natural light. You can counter this by choosing a lightly tinted beige or a pale grey for your walls and ceiling, particularly if you already have white kitchen units.

PRACTICAL FLOOR SURFACES

Balance pale kitchen walls with a dark, bold floor surface. Stained wood, tiles and stone flags are traditional, hard-wearing surfaces for kitchen floors, but they can be prohibitively expensive. If you want a wooden surface, make sure that it is well varnished and sealed to withstand spillage, and be prepared to have it re-treated every other year. A wide variety of linoleums are now manufactured. As well as being durable and easy to clean, they are also less hard underfoot than traditional kitchen floor surfaces. Remember that a rug laid under a kitchen table can be used as a bridge from the colours of the floor to those used on the walls and table.

LEFT Nothing can transform wooden surfaces as much as a well-chosen paint finish. The pale yellow cupboards of this basement kitchen bring a welcome sense of light and are beautifully complemented by the blue and white blind and tiles. The main colours in the room are chosen from the wind palette.

○ Careful use of space and disciplined use of light, together with natural colours, give this kitchen its distinctive character.

○ Light–painted woodwork maximizes the natural light and creates a sense of spaciousness.

○ An eclectic array of brighter bulb vases on the window sill provide a playful accent among the softer shades.

FAR LEFT Using colours of equal intensity from the fire palette creates a dramatic atmosphere in this modern kitchen. Burnt orange walls complement strong lilac-blue units. Black is used for the worktops and skirting boards, moderating the impact of the two main colours.

LEFT White-painted woodwork maximizes the natural light and creates a sense of space in this kitchen. Plain work units designed in an L-shape separate the cooking from the eating area. The white theme continues in the choice of china, placemats, table napkins and tulips, showing what a difference attention to detail can make.

THE BLUE KITCHEN

For centuries, cobalt blue was used as a traditional colour in kitchens and pantries because this particular shade is repellent to insects. Modern ways of preserving foodstuffs have made considerations such as this less relevant than they once were, but you may like to bear the property of cobalt blue in mind if you are decorating a country kitchen, particularly one in a warm climate.

KITCHEN UNITS

Since the Second World War, the design of kitchens has passed through more changes of fashion than any other room – from the streamlined look of the sixties, with its emphasis on plastics, to the nostalgic, rustic look of the seventies and the rise of the fitted kitchen, now giving way once more to a trend towards free-standing furniture. In all of these variations, a constant factor is the need for smooth surfaces, which provide stable, hygienic worktops.

However, these expanses can create a bland, clinical look, especially in a streamlined modern kitchen. One way of countering this is to use a textured paint treatment for your kitchen units. Another is to choose a wood such as ash or maple. High quality, unpainted wood is pleasing to the eye partly because the natural grain in the wood contributes to a depth of colour and a constant, subtle play of light that is absent from synthetic surfaces.

COLOUR ACCENTS

With the range of options that are now available, the way you design your kitchen will probably be influenced as much by your temperament as your taste in colour. If you are a person who likes your surroundings to be regulated and tidy, a streamlined kitchen, where everything is contained in cupboards, will probably appeal to you more than one where pots and pans, mugs and baskets are hung up for display.

Whichever style you prefer, be aware that the kitchen is an ideal place in which to experiment with colour accents. Use the space between upper and lower wall units for a range of tiles; take advantage of simple, functional objects such as kitchen clocks, biscuit tins and tea towels. Pile rosy apples in a black, lacquer bowl for a dramatic effect; arrange lemons alongside aubergines and courgettes in round baskets for a splash of exoticism; for a more muted display, combine bananas with a mixture of pears and nuts. Hang up bunches of dried flowers and herbs; ropes of coloured candles; strings of garlic. Use the space on top of storage units to display big pieces of pottery and china, such as large vases, meat dishes and soup tureens. All of these accents will lend character to your kitchen without you having to make any permanent changes. A well designed kitchen is colourful without being overpowering; functional without being severe: the kind of space that puts you in mind of good living and makes you look forward to the next meal.

ABOVE A pleated blind is a practical and unobstrusive way of decorating a window. Since it is always pulled up, it maximizes the amount of light allowed in at the same time. The discipline of this blue-and-white checked blind is also heightened by the more opaque colours of the bulb vases displayed below it and by the contrast in both design and texture of the blue-and-white tiles.

ABOVE Natural colours and a rustic stone effect can have the effect of making a storage area seem to recede. Here, the cupboards and walls have both been painted as light stonework, introducing a note of humour as well as softening the many sharp angles and corners.

A COOK'S VIEW

Make a stunning focal point of a kitchen window with a fake Roman blind and a display shelf running across the width of the window.

1. Cut the wooden batten to the exact width of your window frame and mark its position on the wall just above the top of the window recess, using a spirit level and pencil. Screw securely into place. Apply one side of the self-adhesive touch-and-close fastener, cut to the length of the batten.

YOU WILL NEED:

○ Main blind fabric the width of the window frame and approximately half the length of the window

○ Lining fabric to the same dimensions

○ Wooden batten the length of the window frame's width

○ Touch-and-close fastener

○ Wooden dowelling the length of the blind's width

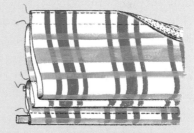

2. Cut out the material, if necessary joining widths together first, to the width of the window frame, adding 2.5cm (1in) on either side for a seam allowance. The length should allow for two or three folds, plus 2.5cm (1in) for turnings at top and bottom. With right sides together, pin and then machine stitch the fabric and lining together on three sides, leaving the top open. Turn to right side out and insert the length of dowelling at the bottom of the blind to weigh it down; stitch to hold it in place. Pin, then slipstitch, the open end to close, folding in 2.5cm (1in) turnings on both main fabric and lining. Sew the other strip of touch-and-close fastener to the top of the blind on the lining side. Fold the fabric to imitate Roman blind folds, as shown, and stitch underneath the folds. Fix the blind in place above the window.

CAROLYN'S TIP

"Fix a wooden shelf across the window recess to create a wonderful display area for glass or other objects, or for a row of indoor plants."

THE BEDROOM

Few experiences are more pleasurable than waking up at leisure in a comfortable, beautifully decorated bedroom.

You do not need to go on holiday, or stay in a smart hotel to enjoy this experience. It is an affordable luxury which can be encountered on an everyday basis by anyone who takes the trouble to introduce colours, textures and bedroom furnishings that please the eye and relax the senses. Successful bedroom design turns as much on skilful use of colour as on any other factor.

The quality that most of us associate with bedrooms is restfulness. Drama certainly plays its part in bedroom design, but in a room that is going to be used every night, the priority is to create a colour scheme which is harmonious, well balanced and elegant.

VERSATILE NATURALS
Naturals are frequently used to excellent effect in bedrooms of all sizes. A subtle blend of pale, natural colours will quickly create an atmosphere of tranquillity. The most frequent error made by inexperienced decorators using naturals is to choose one hue only, and to overlook the effect of its base colour. A natural bedroom soon becomes a bland bedroom if you do not pick up and echo the base colour. For example, with a light grey, which contains black, choose upholstery and curtain fabric that echoes this, however slightly. Pick up an almond natural with dark browns, and a light pink with a deeper scarlet. You can also avoid monotony by introducing a shade which complements the base colour – blue with a yellow-base neutral, pinky red to enhance a green base and orange to enhance a purple base. For a soothing effect, stay with very light tints in your choice of colours; for a note of drama, choose one more strongly coloured item, such as the bedspread or curtains, as a highlight for the room.

You can also introduce variety to a natural bedroom through your choice of textures. Consider hanging blinds

RIGHT Complementary shades of yellow and purple from the fire palette provide the main colours in this room.

○ By using complementary colours on the walls, architectural balance is created in an awkward-shaped room.

○ The foreground colours are more muted, the natural striped fabric of the bedcover echoing and enhancing the slatted woodwork of the bed frame.

○ Another pair of complementary colours, this time red and blue, have been introduced in the two prints on the right hand wall, adding to the spirit of the design.

○ The two pictures side-by-side balance the small window on the adjacent wall.

in a smooth fabric and contrast this with a more loosely woven curtain material, such as calico. Play with different colours and textures by combining different fabrics for your valance, pillowcases, quilt and counterpane. And remember that a layered look will add warmth, so even if you have a wall-to-wall carpet, try laying a rug over it to create this effect.

DARK COLOUR ACCENTS
Rooms that are decorated with peace and quiet in mind can look unimaginative, even if they have been thoughtfully conceived. To add definition and style to a neutral bedroom, introduce a few dark accents, such as wooden or iron curtain poles and bosses, dark mirror frames and an antique bedstead. Avoid heavy woods, however, as their bulk can overpower neutral surroundings.

THE GREEN BEDROOM
The colour of transition and the colour we most readily associate with nature, green is famous for its restful properties, making it an extremely reliable bedroom colour. Another virtue of green is that it appears as a secondary

LEFT Assertive on its own, this warm red from the earth palette becomes more restrained when it is combined with cream from the natural palette. The combination of checks and stripes adds to the visual interest of the room, as does the richly patterned bedside rug.

RIGHT This room is a beautiful example of the use of dark metal for colour accents in a room with a predominantly natural palette. The palest ivory on the wall is taken just a few shades darker with the broadly striped duvet cover, while the intricate lace cushions create an extremely effective contrast to the simplicity of the wrought iron bedstead, chair and mirror.

colour in numerous floral and abstract wallpapers and soft furnishing fabrics. So green will happily combine with many colour schemes in which patterns play a dominant role. Dark green can be too severe in bedrooms, but the mid- to light greens are an excellent foil for floral curtains and bedspreads, or for a highly patterned rug.

SEASONAL CONTRASTS

Before the advent of central heating, it was common practice in many houses to hang warm, interlined curtains and use heavy counterpanes during the winter months, and to replace these with lighter fabrics when spring returned. There is something inherently pleasing about being in a room which has been decorated in keeping with the weather outdoors and the character of the season, even if the indoor temperature is artificially regulated. By changing thick, warm curtains for light cottons and substituting

a heavy bedspread for a pretty lace throw, you can give your bedroom a new lease of life for the summer months without needing to make any structural alterations.

THE BED AS A CENTREPIECE

The type of bed you have, and the way in which you dress it, plays a leading role in creating the atmosphere of your bedroom. Until recently, beds were extremely solid pieces of furniture, which were often sold as part of the contents of the house when it changed hands. Today, such beds are more luxurious than commonplace, but an ordinary divan bed can still become the centrepiece of a bedroom if it is given a fine bedhead and an interesting quilt.

Traditional wooden beds, such as the French country beds, call for solid, traditional colours and old-fashioned counterpanes, such as the patterned quilts that the women of eighteenth- and nineteenth-century North America

made into an art form. The lighter, wooden bed frames that are on the market today call for lighter colours and fabrics such as Indian cottons though, if you prefer it, their wood can be stained to create a darker and more powerful antique effect. For a country look, choose a busy, cottage-garden bedspead or a bright patchwork quilt. For a more restrained, classical atmosphere choose wide, harmonious stripes or a plain colour. For a romantic look, combine a brass bedstead with white sheets, a lace counterpane and a pile of lace-trimmed cushions.

CHOOSING BEDROOM FURNITURE

The position of a bed in a room can make a huge difference to the room's overall appearance. In small bedrooms, the bed will be the dominant piece of furniture, and the colours used in covering it will greatly influence the sense of space in the room. Red makes objects stand out from their surroundings, so if you choose this colour, the size of the bed will appear to increase. On the other hand, if you choose a strong colour for the walls and a lighter shade of the same colour for the bed, the bed will harmonize more discreetly with its surroundings.

Larger rooms can seem to be underfurnished if they contain only a bed and a wardrobe or a chest of drawers. These rooms present the opportunity to create a small seating area. With a large bedroom, consider how you may most effectively divide the space – rugs are a simple but successful way of dividing floor space so as to delineate the different parts of a room.

STORAGE

If you have space, a walk-in wardrobe is an excellent way to store clothes and linen. However, in the majority of contemporary homes, free-standing or fitted wardrobes are

ABOVE Wind colours can create a sunny, welcoming atmosphere, especially when complementary shades are chosen. Here, blue and yellow complement each other beautifully, with wooden furnishings providing a natural accent.

the most commonly used storage systems. The main advantage of fitted cupboards is that they run from floor to ceiling, maximizing storage space. Their drawback is that this can often upset the proportions of a room. One way of countering this is to use special paint effects – pick out the panelling in your cupboard doors in a colour that complements the base colour, introduce a stencil design in the panels, or paint the panels a different colour to the frame of the cupboard. Another attractive option is to choose cupboard frames that are without upper panels and to line them with a simple, patterned fabric. This instantly softens the appearance of a room. You also have the chance to co-ordinate the fabric of the cupboards with the curtains or with other upholstery materials.

A HARLEQUIN PELMET

An unusual pelmet forms part of the curtain treatment in this bedroom and allows colour-coordinated fabrics to be used effectively.

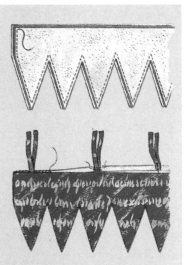

YOU WILL NEED:

○ Pelmet fabric

○ Lining fabric

○ Buckram (stiffened interlining)

○ Brown paper for making a paper pattern

○ Ribbon or tape for pelmet ties, each one approximately 30cm (12in) long and 4cm (1½in) wide

○ Curtain pole

LEFT The mineral palette can come into its own in basement rooms. But the deep reds that establish the signature colour of this bedroom are counterbalanced by natural creams on the curtains, counterpane, lampstands and picture mounts, softening its theatrical quality. Dark blue ropes and lamp shades establish definition and a note of masculinity.

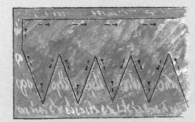

1. Measure the curtain pole to determine the length of the pelmet. Decide on the depth of the pelmet and the proportions of the diamonds and draw the whole pattern on brown paper. Add 1.5cm (⅝in) for a seam allowance all round. Calculate the number of ties required and cut them to length.

CAROLYN'S TIPS

❝ Create a matching bed canopy using the same diamond harlequin pattern: make a half-diamond (a triangle) at each edge of a corner. ❞

❝ As a finishing touch or to add an accent colour, sew a small tassel to the tip of each diamond. ❞

2. Using the paper pattern as a template, cut out the fabric and lining. Cut the buckram 1.5cm (⅝in) smaller all round. Place the right sides of the fabric and lining together, with the buckram in the centre. Pin, tack and then machine-stitch around the diamonds and the sides of the pelmet, leaving the top edge open. Cut along the edge, trimming almost up to the seam line at the lower points of the diamonds and notching the seam allowance at the inward-facing angles. Turn to right side out, using a pencil to push out the points of the diamonds.

3. Mark with pins the position of the ties. Fold the ties in half and pin them in place. Folding in a 1.5cm (⅝in) turning on both fabric and lining, pin and then sew the top edges together by hand or machine, enclosing the ties. Remove the pins. Press the seams, especially the zigzags, then tie the finished pelmet on to the curtain pole.

THE BATHROOM

If we were to decorate other rooms in our homes with the same flair and boldness that we bring to our bathrooms, many of our houses would be a good deal more stylish than they often are.

Whether it is because we spend only short periods of time in them, or because the activity of bathing itself releases our imaginations, we tend as homemakers to bring a more emphatic sense of colour to the decoration of our bathrooms than we do to any other room.

The scale of bathrooms also seems to encourage a sense of adventure. In most contemporary homes, bathrooms take up relatively little space, which makes them good places in which to experiment with colour. If you make a ghastly mistake, it won't cost very much to set it right and start again and a small bathroom can be redecorated in a relatively short space of time, by comparison with most reception rooms.

WATER, LIGHT AND COLOUR

A room which is intended specifically for washing, the bathroom has immediate associations with water. The element of water characteristically changes according to the quality of the light, and reflects the colours of everything around it. The decorating colour which most effectively enhances this play of light and water is turquoise. True turquoise is midway between blue and green in the colour spectrum. Used as a base or a foreground colour, it can be combined with white to create a Mediterranean look, and with coral for a Caribbean look. It can also withstand fiery reds and deep greens, creating a South Pacific atmosphere, and be used with a range of darker blues to emphasize its connection with the sea.

Deep blue and purple are associated with opulence in many cultures, from the lapis lazuli that was prized by the Sumerians and Egyptians to the deep blue glass made by European merchant traders to display their wealth to

RIGHT Cool Scandinavian summers come to mind in the water colours of this simple blue-and-white bathroom.

○ Horizontal, blue-painted wooden panelling around the bath increases the width of the rooms and provides convenient shelf space for a collection of starfish.

○ The graceful white curve of the window is charmingly reflected in the inverted curve of the bath shelf to its left.

○ Dark blue tongue-and-groove paintwork on the side of the bath and the basin cabinet offset the paler panelling above the bath.

○ Blue and white ornaments, a white lampshade and a white chair continue the discipline, making a virtue of simplicity. It is hard to imagine introducing a third colour to this scheme without detracting from the overall effect.

fellow traders. But the starker, more classical blues can appear cold if they are used over large surfaces. A more pleasing effect is often achieved by working with blues that contain a hint of green, taking them closer to turquoise, or of red, which shifts their hue towards purple.

THE WHITE BATHROOM

White is a popular choice for bathrooms, associated as it is not only with light on water but also with cleanliness, and it is the traditional colour for baths, basins and lavatories. One of the chief merits of white is its versatility. Its brilliance can be emphasized by bright chrome or brass fittings and by contrasting dark woods and strong base colours. As a base colour itself, it can be made more playful by introducing bright colour accents with soaps and towels, curtains, blinds and pictures. For a more sophisticated bathroom, use the lightest grey as a wall colour rather than plain white; for a more light-hearted atmosphere choose a light cream, and for a romantic bathroom, white that contains a blush of pink.

ABOVE The rich colours of the mineral palette can turn an ordinary bathroom into something special. Here, the matt finish of the stonework-effect walls contrasts effectively with the sheen of the tiles behind the bath.

across the ceiling as well as the walls. Before you invest in wallpaper for a bathroom, check with the retailer to ensure that it is steam-proof and washable, otherwise you may need to apply a coat of matt varnish to the walls.

ENSUITE BATHROOMS

An ensuite bathroom can either contrast or harmonize with the bedroom to which it connects. Whichever is your preference, take care when you are selecting your bathroom colours to compare them to the bedroom colours on a sample board. A small bathroom alongside a more spacious bedroom involves a significant shift of scale and if you combine this with too dramatic a shift of colour, you may create a contrast that is more overpowering than you intend.

STONEWORK WALLS

The mystery of ancient civilizations is evoked in the rustic *trompe l'oeil* stonework finish to the walls of this bathroom, shown in close-up detail, left. Careful blending of the three colours chosen from the mineral palette creates an authentic stone effect. Use a natural sponge to blend the colours together.

YOU WILL NEED:

○ Graph paper

○ Long and short steel rulers

○ Spirit level

○ Eggshell paint for basecoat

○ Scumble glaze in 3 colours (here, mineral shades of red, terracotta and brown)

○ 2 natural sea sponges, one cut into 3 pieces

○ Low-tack masking tape 50mm (¼in) wide

○ Small paintbrush

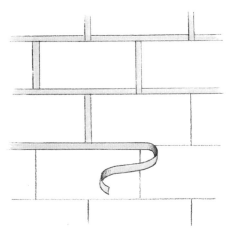

1. Apply two coats of eggshell basecoat paint to the walls, using a roller, and allow to dry. Measure your walls and work out the stonework pattern to scale on graph paper, staggering the joints. As a rough guide, standard stone blocks are 30cm (1ft) high and 60cm (2ft) wide; try to use only whole or half blocks across a row. Transfer the scaled-up measurements to the walls using the steel ruler, spirit level and a pencil. Mask off the edges of each complete block with masking tape.

2. Rinse the sponges in cold water and squeeze out excess water. Using a separate piece of sponge for each colour, dab on a random mix of all three stonework colours, overlapping the patches of colour. Start from the top and work down. While still wet, use the sponge and paintbrush to blend the colours together to create the stonework effect. Do each block in turn. The more random the effect of each block, the greater the illusion of natural stone.

CAROLYN'S TIPS

❝ Paint the basecoat a beige/yellow colour to give the grouting a realistic touch. ❞

❝ For a more 'antique' look, hand-drawn lines can be added using a thin artist's brush to give the effect of cracks in the stone. ❞

❝ Colours from the natural palette combine to give an effective 'stone-coloured' wall – look at natural stone- and brickwork for inspiration. ❞

3. Once you have finished all the blocks and the paint is dry, carefully remove the masking tape to reveal instant 'grouting lines'. If wished, apply two coats of a matt-finish, clear varnish for protection.

CHILDREN'S ROOMS

The customized decoration of children's rooms is a relatively recent phenomenon. Historically, children were perceived for centuries as 'little adults' and while items of furniture such as cots, chairs and desks were made to scale for children, the notion of a particular decorative style for children's rooms, as for children's clothes, did not gain currency until the Victorian period.

Since that time, a steadily increasing range of enchanting wallpapers and furnishing fabrics have been produced with the world of the child in mind. To some extent, this movement has now been bastardized by the widespread merchandising of children's characters on soft furnishing products. Even so, today's parents face a multitude of options in decorating a child's room.

INFANCY

Infancy is traditionally associated with white, as the colour representing new life and innocence. With a newborn baby, it is difficult not to be captivated by the prospect of a tiny cradle with fine white drapes. It is as though the magical quality of the first months of life is somehow extended by placing the baby in surroundings that are specifically intended to celebrate its arrival. Magic aside, an advantage to using white as the base colour in a newborn baby's nursery is that you can easily paint over it as the child grows and you want to introduce stronger themes. If white seems too plain, try choosing a pale pastel colour and providing interest with a wallpaper or stencil frieze, patterned curtains and a crewel rug.

Although newborn babies cannot focus properly, they do sense the quality of their surroundings from a very early age. So take the trouble to prepare your baby's room in advance of the birth, and aim to create a colour scheme which you feel will provide your baby with a sense of security and well-being. Modern babies seem to acquire a great

RIGHT Busy patterns, brightly painted woodwork and a warm background colour, all from the earth palette, set the tone for this girl's bedroom.

○ A lick of paint – cream, red and pale blue – has transformed the bedside table and chest of drawers, while fabric panels in the same colours give a facelift to the wardrobe.

○ Three fabrics with contrasting patterns and harmonizing colours combine to create subtle and playful contrasts between the curtains, blinds and bed covers.

○ The warmth that is inherent in the red of this fabric is amplified by the red paintwork on the walls. A quite different atmosphere would have been created with blue or yellow paint.

○ With these busy fabric designs, the simplest coir matting easily suffices as floorcovering.

deal of apparatus within the first weeks of life and many stores now offer customized nursery sets comprising a changing unit, cot and chest of drawers – so you may want to make these items the starting point for your decoration.

PRE-SCHOOL CHILDREN

Pre-school children spend much of their day at home and their bedrooms are as likely to be used for playing in as for sleeping in. During this critical period of your child's growth, your concern is likely to turn around how best to engage your child's interest in the world around him or her. Small children are insatiably curious, and by the age of two they are beginning to develop a conscious sense of pattern, shape and colour. There are all sorts of ways in which you can foster this blossoming awareness, not only with toys but also with patterned wallpapers, playmats, duvet covers and curtains.

There is a widespread assumption that small children most appreciate primary colours and simple patterns, but

LEFT The light green paint that provides the background colour for this bedroom runs right across the ceiling as well as the walls, increasing the sense of space. Green from the water palette is stylishly offset by its complementary colour, red, from the fire palette, on the skirting board, radiator and bed base. But the most notable feature of this bedroom is the window. By using vivid red and yellow stripes on the frame, a red blind and a cheap and cheerful Indian hanging, the creator of this room has turned an ordinary window into a visual feast.

children can have quite a sophisticated sense of colour and pattern from a very early age. If you decorate a toddler's room in raw yellows, reds, and blues, he is likely to be bored by it as soon as you are. If you think back to your own childhood, you may well find that you have a particular memory of the pattern on the wallpaper or a carpet. Young children enjoy intricacy and they live in close contact with the floor. Carpets with interesting lines and curves double as roads, rivers and other exotic landscapes.

Curtains that fall to the floor provide hiding places and create interesting pools of light for a child to explore, while detailed patchwork quilts provide a starting point from which a child can begin to spin his or her own stories.

PRIMARY SCHOOL CHILDREN

Once children are at primary school, they are starting to stake their claim on the look of their room. They may well want to use their bedroom walls for their own paintings,

LEFT Bright fire colours and simple but clever designs make this bedroom an ideal setting for a young child's adventures. A broad frieze lowers the ceiling, bringing the scale of the room down to become more child-centred. *Trompe l'oeil* cubes make the bed into a play area in its own right and cleverly camouflage two drawers.

LEFT Storage space for children's toys presents a challenge that is all too often dealt with by storing the toys out of sight. This bright pattern of cubes from the water palette shows how the challenge can be addressed openly and made into an eye-catching feature of a child's room.

charts and diagrams. Your main concern now is probably that the carpet will be hardwearing and all surfaces easy to clean. For this age group, the decorating that is most appreciated is the kind that fosters imaginative play – making your child a bed that is like a boat, or a wardrobe that doubles as a sentry box, will delight him or her far more than expensive designer curtain fabric. If you do not have the skill or the budget to create a specially designed bed, consider painting your child's furniture. It is very easy to pick up cheap, second-hand chests of drawers that can be transformed by a set of stencils into a jungle or farm-yard scene. A customized piece of furniture can also become a treasured memento of younger days when your child is older.

COLOURS FOR BOYS, COLOURS FOR GIRLS

As a culture, we still associate blue with boys, and pink with girls, despite the fact that these colours may do little or nothing for many children of both sexes. Indeed, it is said that babies notice primary colours first. You can learn about your child's preferences by playing games that involve choosing colours and noticing which are the favourites. For a room that will work well for children of both sexes, avoid stereotypical colours such as pink, and fabrics that are overtly masculine or feminine in their design. Yellow is always a safe choice as a background colour for a small child's room – think of using check or striped curtains that will go with the different furnishings as a child progresses from a cot to a bed. Changing the duvet cover is always a simple and quick way of giving the room a new look. Abstract patterns, or animal patterns, combined with rich, earthy colours are entirely appropriate for children of both sexes.

TEENAGERS

Her bedroom is more often than not the only part of the house that your teenager can claim as her own. It will be her sanctuary; the place to which she retreats to plan and to read; to rock the house with music and to conspire with her friends. Whatever your notion of the perfect teenage bedsit, you can be sure that your child will have strong views on the matter as well. Let her have her say. To be adolescent is to experiment, so if your thirteen-year-old daughter wants lime green and orange cubes on her bedroom walls, she will have her own special reasons for that choice. If your sixteen-year-old son insists that his bedroom is painted deep purple, it may be simplest to let him have his own way.

With children of any age, decorating can raise so many issues that the room goes to the bottom of your priorities and remains unchanged, year after year. Try not to let the difficulties drive you into opting out altogether. A very simple idea, such as a frieze round the dado of a pre-school child's bedroom, or floral curtains and a proper dressing table for a ten-year-old girl, will help them to appreciate and enjoy their own space and to feel valued and special at the same time.

CAROLYN'S TIP

❝ Do not worry if some images seem darker than others. Leave it until the border is completed and take an overall view of the wall. Any obvious differences can always be corrected, but bear in mind that these variations can give a charming, hand-finished look to your work. ❞

HOME SWEET HOME

This stencilled frieze takes inspiration from the design on the rug, using reversed colours. The frieze lowers the ceiling and lends interest to what would otherwise be quite a stark white wall space. The choice of blue from the wind palette with natural white creates a crisp but at the same time inviting atmosphere. Warmth is added by the golden tones of the wooden furnishings and floorboards.

YOU WILL NEED:

○ Ready-made stencil (or you can make your own to echo a motif in the room)

○ Low-tack masking tape

○ Non-drip stencil paints

○ A stencil brush for each colour

○ Steel ruler

○ Spirit level

○ Pencil

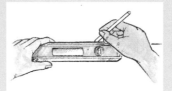

1. Work out where you are going to place the stencil. Try to line it up with something in the room, such as the curtain pole here. Using the steel rule and spirit level, mark pencil lines on the wall to ensure that your frieze runs in a straight line.

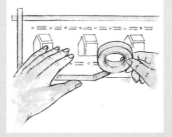

2. Stick the stencil to the wall with masking tape around the edges. Start in the centre of the wall and work to the right and then to the left corners. Work out how many images will fit between the centre and the corner; alway leave more space between the last few images to fill a small gap to a corner, rather than using half an image.

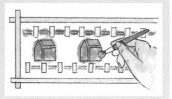

3. Using the stencil brush, fill in the main colour (blue) first, moving the stencil along the wall as you complete each one. It may be possible to paint another colour at the same time, using a different brush, provided it is not adjacent to the main colour. Try to ensure that no paint goes under the stencil.

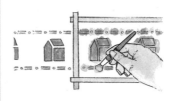

4. Once the first colour is dry, line up the stencil again and fill in the next colour (here, ochre), using a separate stencil brush.

THE HOME OFFICE

Economic benefits such as reduced rent, lower overheads and no commuting has made working from home, on either a part- or a full-time basis, an increasingly attractive option for many people.

The post-war era has seen a major shift from an industrialized world to one which is more and more dominated by information technology. This revolution is enabling a growing number of individuals to communicate long-distance from desktop to desktop in a way that is unprecedented.

PLANNING PERMISSION AND SAFETY REGULATIONS

Before you embark on the conversion of a particular room or outbuilding into a home office, it is essential to check your local trading laws. Some suburban district councils simply do not allow the practice of certain businesses from home if they are likely to disrupt the peace of the neighbourhood. If you will have to extend your home to make an office space, make sure that you have the appropriate planning permission before you start.

Once you are registered as working from home, industrial health and safety standards will apply. Take the trouble to find out what the requirements are, both on your own account and also on behalf of anyone you may be employing to work from your home.

SPACE AND COLOUR

If you are working or plan to work from home, a primary consideration will be space. You may be fortunate enough to live in a house that has plenty of room to spare for the creation of a home office, but if this is not the case, choosing a room to work in will probably mean sacrificing a bedroom or reception room. For most professionals, work involves three different space requirements: space for undisturbed work, space for meetings and space for the storage of documents. You can go out of the home for

RIGHT If you work from home, it is well worth taking the trouble to design an office that is comfortable as well as practical. Warm wind colours have been used to create this stylish home office.

❍ Streamlined wooden furniture and shelving creates a natural, uncluttered look.

❍ Pale paintwork on the walls and ceiling continue the natural theme in a simple and unobtrusive way.

❍ Coir matting provides a practical, hardwearing floor surface that harmonizes with the wooden furniture.

❍ The upper bookshelf runs right round the room, making good use of what would otherwise be wasted space.

❍ The wide, floral blind introduces a feminine note.

❍ The same floral fabric is repeated on the cushion of the armchair, which hints at comfort.

LEFT Dark and light earth colours work together in this tiny study. A modest alcove has become a workplace in its own right with the introduction of a magnificent antique bureau and matching bookcase. The pale lemon walls offset the dark wood of the bureau and the trunk opposite it, while the patterns on the ikat-weave rug, paisley lampshade and pelmet break up the areas of solid colour.

RIGHT A natural background palette with red accents from the fire palette give this home office a crisp and streamlined appearance. A grey carpet and white on the walls and ceiling increase the sense of space and the splashes of red introduce brightness and warmth.

storage, and if you have company documents you should do so to protect them from fire; you may also be able to run your professional life so that you do not have meetings from home. If you do want to use the house for occasional meetings, consider letting your dining room double as a conference room.

In a house with limited space, it can be tempting to choose the smallest room as the office. This has many advantages: your heat, light and power bills will be correspondingly lower and if you are the kind of person who likes to work in a cocoon, having a small, cosy workplace can be very pleasant. On the other hand, if you enjoy and need plenty of room in which to spread out, you will probably regret trying to squeeze all of your work material into a tiny attic or basement, particularly if you are working from home on a full-time basis.

When you are setting yourself up at home, it pays to

think ahead. How much space will you need three years from now? It is better to start with lots of space and steadily fill it, than to find you have to move to another part of the house to give yourself the space you need.

Corporate offices tend to be severe and clinical environments, but it is increasingly being recognized that people perform better in an atmosphere which affords some expression of character. Most office equipment will do little to improve the aesthetics of your workplace, so you need to make the most of any opportunities you have to introduce a sense of style to your surroundings. In a small room, you will probably need every inch of space for work-related material. Even so, you can create a play of colour by using contrasting colours for bookshelves and the wallspace behind them, hanging lots of pictures close together on any free wall space, and laying a kelim or dhurrie on the floor.

LEFT Sewing is an activity which requires a strong light source. Here, cool air colours and lightweight blinds maximize the natural light, while the choice of yellow as the signature colour imbues the whole room with a sunny atmosphere.

In a larger office, it is possible to introduce bold colour statements and add comfort with pictures, prints or mirrors on the walls, an interesting array of objects on the mantelpiece and scatter cushions on an easy chair or sofa. For a warm, womb-like atmosphere, choose a base colour that is dark, such as a deep red, green or burnt orange, and complement it with a dark wooden desk and shelving units. For a more airy atmosphere, stay with naturals and restrict darker colours to the floor. As in other rooms, bear in mind that an office with plenty of natural light will look well painted in a bright or neutral colour, while a darker space will respond well to deeper shades.

WINDOW TREATMENTS

However small your office, you can introduce a degree of individuality through the kind of window treatment you choose. Curtains will take up more space than blinds, though they will also make the room less formal. If you have a period home, you may be able to decorate fitted shutters; in a more modern house, you can choose from a wide variety of blinds. One of the pleasures of having a blind is that you can use it to create a play of light in the daytime, depending on the level to which you draw it down. If you have fabrics or books in your office that will fade with exposure to sunlight, a blind will be practical as well as decorative.

If you do work from home, you will spend more time in your office than in any other part of the house. A comfortable workplace will make a significant difference to the quality of your life. So it is well worth going to a little extra trouble and expense to make your home office a room that you actively enjoy.

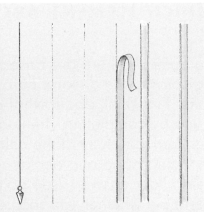

1. Apply two coats of basecoat paint with a roller or paintbrush and allow it to dry. Beware of making the stripes too narrow or the overall effect will be very busy (the stripes here are about 15cm/6in wide). Then measure the width of the wall and divide it evenly into the stripes. Using the chalked plumb-line, mark out the stripes by snapping it against the wall or use a conventional plumb-line and draw a dotted line with a pencil. Apply masking tape to butt up to the edges of the coloured stripes.

PAINTED STRIPED WALLS

The effect of bright yellow stripes painted on a white background makes a striking wall pattern at a fraction of the cost of wallpaper.

CAROLYN'S TIPS

" Try painting two different but harmonious shades of the same colour for a soft, two-dimensional tonal effect. "

" Omit the masking tape and rely on your eye and a steady brush-stroke if you want your stripes to have a more hand-finished edge. "

YOU WILL NEED:

○ Emulsion basecoat paint for the walls

○ Roller or paintbrush

○ Emulsion paint colour for the stripes

○ Wide paintbrush

○ Chalk plumb-line or plumb-line and pencil

○ Low-tack masking tape

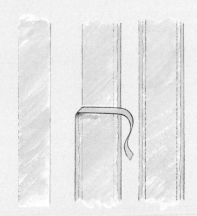

2. Paint every alternate strip with the stripe-colour, using the wide paintbrush. Start at the top and work downwards, making swift brush-strokes. Take care not to overlap the edges of the masking tape. When the paint is dry, carefully remove the masking tape.

WHICH ELEMENT ARE YOU?

The questions here are based on the kind of choices anyone decorating a home has to make. First think about what colour means to you by completing The Real You (below). Then look carefully at the colour choices on the facing page and decide which you prefer. Your answers (see page 128) will determine whether you should select warm- or cool- based palettes for your colour schemes. Turn back to the colour sections on pages 22-61, looking at either the warm or the cool colour wheels. The palette with most of the colours you like to live with determines your element – Air, Wind, Water, Fire, Earth or Mineral. Naturals can be used with all the palettes or on their own.

THE REAL YOU

1. What are your favourite colours?

....

2. What are your least favourite colours?

....

3. How important is home decoration to you?

....

4. Look at the colours you live with now: are you happy with them?

....

5. Are there some colours you prefer to live with?

....

6. Do you find yourself always choosing the same colours?

....

7. Have you ever wanted a room in a particular colour, and then found you did not like it?

....

8. If you had decorated a room you were not satisfied with, could you live with it or would you feel it had to be changed?

....

9. Which decorating style do you feel happiest in?

....

10. Do the colours in your home reflect some of the colours you like to wear?

....

1. Natural tones are simple and understated. Which of these shades would you choose?

2. You are looking for a versatile, neutral colour for the carpet of a hall and staircase. Which of the these do you prefer?

3. Reds create a dramatic and stimulating effect in halls and dining rooms. Which of these shades most appeals to you?

4. Blue rooms can be very restful. Which of these blues would you prefer to use in a blue colour scheme?

5. You want to introduce green fabrics into your living room colour scheme. Which green would you select?

6. You want to brighten up a dark kitchen. Which of these yellows would you prefer to cook with?

7. Which of these colours would you find most restful to sleep with?

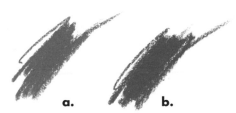

8. Introducing bright colours to a white room creates a bright, Mediterranean atmosphere. Which would you choose as the main colour?

9. You are decorating a guest room with a pink theme. On which of these shades would you base the colour scheme?

10. You love the aqua colours of the sea. Which shade appeals to you most?

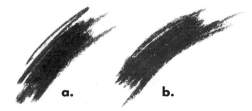

11. You have a dining room to decorate and want to reflect the colour of red wine. Which do you prefer?

12. Choose which of these two colours you prefer.

Turn to page 128 for the answers.

INDEX

Acknowledgments

AUTHOR'S ACKNOWLEDGMENTS

Writing this book and developing the *Living with Colour* concept has been the most fascinating voyage of discovery into the world of colour. Many people have helped and contributed to my work and research. My special thanks go to: Tessa Strickland, my co-author, for her unique skill in interpreting my thoughts and words; Jill Strieder for her constant encouragement and advice; Suzi Pickles for teaching me all about colour analysis; Anthony Evans for his invaluable assistance in researching fabric sources; Ruth Churchman for her insight into colour.

I would also like to thank the following fabric manufacturers: Malabar, Colefax & Fowler, and Bernard Thorp for the fabrics used in my living room (page 84), C.F. Deanswood Ltd. for making the curtains and upholstery; Jane Churchill Ltd. for the dining-room tablecloth fabric (page 93); Colefax & Fowler for the kitchen-blind fabric (page 99), as well as M.S. Bloomfield Ltd for the kitchen units.

This book would not have been possible without the wonderful support of our literary agent, Maggie Noach, and Polly Powell and the team at HarperCollins. I am also very grateful to Nancy Traversy for letting us take photographs in her beautiful home.

A special debt of gratitude goes to Sue Hoggard for all her support and for looking after Jamie and Geordie so brilliantly. A big thank you too to Paula and Claire for all their help. Nothing, however, would have been possible without the love, guidance and inspiration of Francis – the best husband I could ever have.

CAROLYN WARRENDER'S WORKSHOPS

This book aims to open your eyes to what you can achieve in your home by using the colours that are right for you. You can now see the book come alive by attending a one-day Carolyn Warrender *Living with Colour* workshop, where you will gain further inspiration and colour-scheming expertise. You will also have the opportunity to discuss your plans with Carolyn Warrender, who will give you money-saving tips and teach you tricks of the trade. You will be given your personalized *Living with Colour* file containing colour samples, a shopping directory and helpful hints, as well as space for you to plan your own budgets and colour schemes.

The *Living with Colour* system is also available by mail order. For further information, fill in the form on the back flap of the book's jacket, or a photocopy of it, and send an A5 stamped, self-addressed envelope to:
Carolyn Warrender Ltd., Living with Colour Workshops/Mail Order/Stencils (delete as applicable), P.O. Box 360, London SW1V 4EJ (tel./fax 0171-821 5661).

WHICH ELEMENT ARE YOU?

Answers to the questions on pages 124-5:
If most of your answers are **A**s, you are a warm-based person, and should use colours which have yellow undertones. The warm colour wheels reflect your colours. If most of your answers are **B**s, this means you are a cool-based person and should use colours with blue undertones, as illustrated in the cool colour wheels.

Now turn to pages 20-56 and look at the warm and cool colour wheels in all the different palettes. The one which contains the greatest number of colours you would like to use in your home determines which 'element' you are.

However, it is important to feel free to mix and match, to use colours from other palettes too. If you are cool and like a particular warm colour, or vice versa, then use it for details and accents.

PICTURE CREDITS

The Publishers wish to thank the following photographers and organizations for their kind permission to reproduce the following images:

Robin Allison Smith 14(b); Laura Ashley 30, 115(t); Bauhaus-Archiv 10; Camera Press 54, 75, 90, 118-9, 122; Crowson Fabrics Ltd 113; Wendy A Cushing Ltd 120-1; The English Stamp Company 48-9; Robert Harding Syndication/IPC Magazines 18, 24-5, 56-7, 67, 68-9, 80-1, 84-5, 132-3; The Interior Archive/Simon Brown 49, 82, 83, 85, 92/James Mortimer 14(cl), 91/Fritz Von Der Schulenburg 8-9, 12-13, 20-1, 36-7, 44, 52-3, 104-5, 106, 124-5, 128-9, 136-7/ (Kath Kidson) 17/ (Dot Spikings) 25(r), 97/ (Richard Mudditt) 25, 31/ (Nessa O'Neill) 37/ (Mimmi O'Connell) 66/ (K H Scherer) 71/ (Julia Boston) 88-9/ (Juliette Mole) 114/ (Richard Hudson) 123/ Christopher Simon Sykes 15(tl)/ Woloszynski 43, 55, 64, 70, 102, 120; Maison de Marie Claire/Gilles de Chabaniex/ C de Chabaniex/ Bastit 40-1 & 91, Gaillard/ Comte Moireau 116-17; Mulberry/Guy Hervais 60; Mike Newton 12(t), 14(cr&tl), 15(b), 68, 121; David Parmiter 98; David Phelps 24, 69, 76, 101; Ianthe Ruthven 84-5; Christian Sarramon (Masurel) 19; Elizabeth Whiting & Associates (Peter Wolozynski) 1, 16/ Coté Sud (C Dugied) 109/ Coté Sud (Y Duronsoy) 11/ Coté Sud (B Touillon) 10 & 77/ Coté Ouest (J Darblay)/Rodney Hyatt 96 & 116-17/Di Lewis 14(tr) & 42/ Michael Nicholson 12(b) & 15(tr).

The following photographs were specially taken for HarperCollins by Shona Wood: 20, 26, 32, 38, 44, 48, 50, 78, 80-1, 83, 84, 86, 92-3, 94-5, 98-9, 103, 104, 108, 110, 115(b).